MW00354661

MOMS
of the Missing

Living the Nightmare

STEFFEN HOU

©2019 Steffen Hou. All rights reserved. No part of this publication may be reproduced, distributed, or transmitted in any form or by any means, including photocopying, recording, or other electronic or mechanical methods, without the prior written permission of the author, except in the case of brief quotations embodied in critical reviews and certain other noncommercial uses permitted by copyright law.

ISBN: 978-1-54397-972-5 (print)

ISBN: 978-1-54397-973-2 (ebook)

This book is written in loving memory of all the children who have lost their lives at the hands of a vicious kidnapper, and is dedicated to those who are still held captive. Perhaps someone reading this book will remember a small but important detail about one of the abductions described in these pages and will come forward with new information that will lead to the safe recovery of one of the missing.

CONTENTS

PROLOGUE:
A VOICE FOR THE VICTIMS

BLOK 70

The man approached without making a sound, and I did not notice him until it was too late.

Quickly, he put me in a choke hold, grabbing my neck, and pressed the gun against my temple.

"Walk," he commanded in a menacing voice.

As he forced me down the dirt road with a firm grip around my neck, I slowly realised what was happening. I was being taken by a stranger.

The incident happened in Blok 70. A part of the Serbian capital of Belgrade where human traffickers forced illegal immigrants into involuntary labour before transporting them over the borders into the European Union. The year was 2001. The civil war in the Balkans had just ended, leaving the region in chaos, without law and order. The Serbian capital was a mecca for criminals; human traffickers took advantage of the lawless situation.

I had been investigating human trafficking in the area for a while when the man forced me to go with him. The traffickers wanted to prevent me from contacting the illegal immigrants who worked in the mall where I was taken.

When I felt the cold steel of the gun against my skin, I also felt fear: the man immediately ordered that we start running, and as he continued to press the gun against my temple, I was afraid one of us might stumble and the gun would go off by mistake.

The farther we ran, the more alone I felt. Instinctively, I felt a need for someone to be there to comfort me. A friend or a total stranger, it didn't matter. I just didn't want to be alone with my fear of dying at the hands of a criminal.

When we were out of sight behind some work sheds, the man, who was in his mid-twenties, commanded me to stop. By which he meant not only that I should stop running but that I should also end my enquiries into human trafficking. Otherwise, he would be happy to end them for me, he said, pointing the gun to my head.

Being taken at gunpoint affected me deeply. In the incident's aftermath, I suffered symptoms resembling those of post-traumatic stress disorder (PTSD). I was constantly scared, and I had flashbacks. I would walk down the peaceful streets of my hometown in Denmark—far from the brutality of Serbia—and suddenly have a quick vision of someone grabbing me from behind and holding me at gunpoint. The inner turmoil persisted for years.

When I was forced out of the mall several people had witnessed what happened. Yet none of them had done anything to help me. They were probably concerned with their own well-being and were too afraid to get involved. However, their inaction greatly affected me. I felt very disappointed in humanity. For a while I lost the trust I had in others.

The incident in Serbia probably lasted fifteen minutes. In this frightening and stressful situation, I lost track of time. However, I know my experience cannot be compared to more heinous crimes where people are abducted and held hostage for days, weeks, years—or even decades. But five or ten or fifteen or twenty minutes is a long time when you are fearing for your life. I have experienced how scared you instinctively feel as a human being when someone physically grabs you and orders you to come with them. I know how alone you are.

That is the reason I decided to write this book. I want to give the victims a voice.

AN EPIDEMIC OF MISSING PEOPLE

In addition to the impetus provided by the lingering effects of my incident with the man in Blok 70, the idea for this book was nursed along after working on another project in America a few years ago. While investigating illegal immigration, I met numerous girls who were forced into prostitution at massage parlors in New York City, Los Angeles, and Miami. They were forced to pay off their debts to human traffickers by engaging in commercial sex acts.

However, as I discovered, not all girls working at brothels and massage parlors are illegal immigrants. Many are young ladies abducted from American streets or lured into sex trafficking by people they once trusted and believed to be a friend or a lover. Examining their stories also lead me to investigate the general problem of abduction in the United States, with a special focus on children and adolescents—a problem some describe as "an epidemic of missing people".

Every year, almost 425,000 children are reported as missing to law enforcement agencies in the United States.

In *Moms of the Missing: Living the Nightmare* I tell the stories of ten American parents whose children have been abducted—and in one "worst case" scenario, killed—by a neighbour, a paedophile, or a serial killer. Through heartbreaking interviews the parents describe the uncertainty and pain of not knowing where their children are, or if they are even still alive.

Many of the parents shared their story with me in the hopes of creating a safer tomorrow, one in which other parents can prevent their children from becoming victims. Other parents featured in this book told their stories because even though their happy life turned into a nightmare within a few seconds, they still believe miracles can happen in a heartbeat. Perhaps someone reading this book who knows something about a child's abduction will come forward with important information that will lead to the child's recovery....

However, these sorts of miracles do not happen for everyone. Too many of the parents in this book have experienced the unbelievable cruelty of having a child murdered, and the unconsolable grief that accompanies the child's fate. Still, they have shared their stories to give parents who are searching for a missing child hope. These strong survivors also describe how a parent, after having been the victim of the worst possible crime, can still reclaim their life, although that life will forever be a different life.

To provide a comprehensive accounting of how kidnappings affect both the individual victim and the entire victim's family, I have also interviewed two people who survived their kidnapper's crimes. When Alicia Kozakiewicz was thirteen years old, she was one of the first children in the United States to be "groomed" and abducted by an internet predator. Law enforcement told Alicia's parents that their chances of getting Alicia back alive were one in a million. But the miracle did happen: Alicia returned safely to her family. Today, Alicia is a young woman who advocates for child safety. In this book she describes the nightmare she lived while trapped in a dungeon. She sheds light on what goes through the heart and head of a kidnapped child. She also describes how a victim, after recovery, can restore both life and love.

Rhonda Stapley was also the victim of a kidnapper. Forty-five years ago she was abducted and raped by serial killer Ted Bundy. Her miracle happened when she seized her one chance to escape. For almost four decades she remained quiet about her abduction, but today she tells her story willingly, in the hopes of motivating present and future victims to report their crimes. She believes that doing so may prevent them from experiencing the same pain as she did. Had she only told the truth and asked for help when she escaped, she might not have suffered from decades of PTSD. She also describes how she harbors guilt for having escaped alive while other women became victims of Ted Bundy. If she had reported her abduction, perhaps law enforcement would have caught the notorious kidnapper and killer much earlier than they did.

Finally, a mother whose child was recovered provides a letter of hope for families still searching for their children. However, the letter is not only a message of hope; it is also an insightful offering describing how parents can move on with life once they have their loved ones back.

MAGNIFICENT MOMS

I have divided this book into chapters describing the different types of child abductions, how the abductions happen, who the victims and abductors often are, and, not least in importance, the magnitude of the problem. I have categorised the different types of abductions as:

- *Stranger abductions*
- *Human trafficking abductions*
- *Family abductions*
- *Infant abductions*
- *Long-term abductions*

I also describe the danger sex offenders pose to children, how kids are lured by online predators, and how domestic violence can deteriorate into an abduction with a fatal outcome. But I also wish to generate hope by describing how victims can fight back and, not least of all, how abductions can be prevented.

While writing this book, I came to learn that mothers are often more likely than fathers to talk about their pain and loss. The men I contacted were more reluctant to tell their stories because they felt they failed by not being able to protect their children. Their sense of failure made it more difficult for them to talk about their emotions and ordeals. In all fairness it should be mentioned that the fathers of abducted children also tirelessly fight to bring home their children; they sacrifice everything to make that happen. But because of their reluctance I chose to primarily interview mothers, which explains the title of this book: *Moms of the Missing: Living the Nightmare*.

According to the FBI's National Crime Information Center (NCIC) there are currently more than 88,000 active missing persons records in the United States. People under the age of eighteen account for more than 32,000 of these records. Here are some of their stories, along with the story of Alicia Kozakiewicz, whose experience is not least in importance, for she, too, was once one of these records.

1

A SURVIVOR'S MISSION

A HUMAN ISSUE

The Abducted: Alicia Kozakiewicz
Date of Birth: 03/23/1988
Missing From: Pittsburgh, Pennsylvania
Abducted: 01/01/2002 (13 years old)
Classification: Endangered Missing

As a child, Alicia always carried a doll. Sometimes an armless doll, other times a doll that was headless. Her mother, Mary, was often uncomfortable with the indifference Alicia exhibited toward the condition of her dolls. She felt it was embarrassing that Alicia preferred to play with broken toys. Although she gladly offered to buy her daughter new dolls, Alicia always declined.

"I did not want new dolls because my 'handicapped dolls', as I called them, needed my love more," Alicia says now.

Caring for those dolls exemplified Alicia's character and personality. Even as a young girl, she always offered a word of comfort, a hug of support, or a helping hand, no matter if it was for an elderly person carrying grocery bags or supporting a friend with a broken heart. For example, every Wednesday, Alicia and her family would go to the local skating rink, where she often found herself playing the role of peace-maker between her peers.

"It meant a lot to me, making other people feel happy. I had so much love in my life that I wanted to make the world a better place and share my joy with the world," Alicia says.

She recalls that as a child, she dreamt of becoming a teacher who would guide kids safely through life; or an astronaut, discovering new planets where people would live in harmony.

"I was a sweet, silly, gentle, and kind child," Alicia says about that period in her life, when the blue-eyed girl still had not realised that kindness can be dangerous.

On New Year's Day of 2002, Alicia was having dinner with her family at their house in Pittsburgh. The dinner was one of the most important times of the year. The family always had the same holiday meal to celebrate life—and each other.

"We had pork and sauerkraut. It was our way of welcoming the New Year and wishing each other good luck," she says.

As the family was finishing their meal on the first day of 2002, their luck was about to be tested.

When her parents cleared the table and prepared to serve dessert, Alicia said she had a stomachache. The thirteen-year-old asked her mother if she could lie down. But instead of going to her room, Alicia slipped past the Christmas tree in the hall and snuck out the front door to meet a friend.

Alicia knew the friend only from online chat sessions, but tonight her friend had asked her to come out of her house so they could meet in person and wish each other a Happy New Year. And, as it was in Alicia's nature to accommodate her friends' wishes, she said yes—without her parents' permission. After all, she was going to be away for only a few minutes, and she would be back in time for dessert, walnut apple pie.

The wind bit Alicia's face when she opened the door. The temperature outside was below zero, and Alicia was not wearing a coat as she left the house. When she reached the bottom of the driveway she was shivering. Still, she would make an effort to fulfill her friend's expectations.

Alicia walked the block from her parents' house, on a street covered with ice. Falling crystals stung her face relentlessly as she waited for her friend to show up. Somehow she felt relieved that he was not already there. Although she was curious to meet her online friend, she was also nervous. Suddenly she had an intuitive feeling that something was terribly wrong.

"I remember the total silence. Nobody was outside in the freezing night. Then I heard a voice; my intuition spoke up and said, 'Alicia, what are you doing? This is dangerous. Go home now', " she recalls.

Quickly Alicia decided to turn around to go home; but just as she did, she heard an actual voice calling, 'Alicia?'.

"I don't remember walking over to the car, but suddenly I was in it. I immediately knew I was in danger. I got so scared when the monster grabbed my hand and crushed it. I started crying, but no one could hear me. Then the man barked commands at me. He told me that he had cleaned out the trunk of the car and if I didn't stop crying, he would put me in it," Alicia explains.

When the teenage girl walked out of her parents' house she had expected to meet a friend—at least, a friend from the online world. In reality, she was now facing a dangerous paedophile who had come to kidnap Alicia and turn her into his sex slave.

For the next five hours he drove through Pennsylvania and crossed the state line, driving into Virginia.

"In the beginning I recognised all the street names as he drove past [them]. Then suddenly I didn't know the street names and I couldn't even recognise where he had taken me. It seemed like he drove forever, and I was terrified," Alicia says.

She regained hope when he reached a tollbooth. Before pulling up to the tollbooth, the abductor had threatened her and told her to stay quiet. However, Alicia was sure the tollbooth attendant would notice the crying, scared child sitting in the car. But he did not. Alicia's abductor sped off.

"People in tollbooths and ground transportation were not yet trained to recognise potentially dangerous situations, such as child abductions or human trafficking," Alicia notes.

For the remainder of the drive, Alicia sat paralysed, too afraid to say a word. Her thoughts became darker and more hopeless the farther her abductor drove her from her home and away from the people who would be able to save her: her parents.

Back at home, Alicia's family had already grown horribly concerned about where their daughter might be. Earlier, when dessert was ready, Alicia's older brother had gone upstairs to summon her, but Alicia was nowhere to be seen. Trying to rationalise their daughter's absence, Alicia's parents suspected she might be teasing them by playing hide-and-seek. The family searched closets…under beds…in every corner of the house. When they stepped out the front door, they saw no telltale footprints in the snow and ice: the wind had swept her footprints away, just as the abductor had swept Alicia from her family. The parents had no way of knowing their daughter was trapped in a stranger's car, fearing her abductor would pull over any moment and kill her.

"It was a long, terrifying ride to the unknown. I expected to die horribly. When he got to his home his fat, sweaty hands grabbed and squeezed mine as he took me through the house and down to his basement. There was a padlock on the door, and when he opened it, he forced me into his dungeon," Alicia says.

HOUSE OF HORROR

The basement windows had been painted black so no one could look into the cold, dark dungeon filled with sadistic torture devices. Over the course of the next several days, the abductor repeatedly used those horrors on the young and helpless girl.

"He immediately removed my clothing, looked at me and said, 'This is going to be really hard for you,' and that it was okay if I cried. He then put a locking dog collar around my neck. Afterwards I was repeatedly beaten, starved, tortured, and raped. It was a nightmare that had become a terrible reality. To survive, I knew I had to make him believe that I would do whatever he told me to do....It is a horrible dilemma for a child to face: wanting to cry, and fight, but at the same time, also having to think about what you must say, and do, to keep yourself alive. I was focused on getting through, just surviving, to the next minute. I could not imagine the next hour. I just had to get through it minute by minute," Alicia explains.

For four days she was held captive. It was impossible to escape her torturer; she tried several times. In one struggle, her nose was broken. The kidnapper enjoyed torturing the little girl. He would hang Alicia, her arms bound above her head, while beating her. Afterwards he would attach clamps to her, using them as conduits to send bolts of electricity through Alicia's tiny, eighty-four-pound body. When he was done physically torturing the defenceless child, he attached the dog collar around Alicia's neck to a heavy chain, preventing her from escaping. As Alicia lay bolted to the floor she could do little more than await the abductor's next attack.

On the fourth day of captivity, the kidnapper fed Alicia for the first time. But he once again threatened her.

"That morning, he told me he was returning to work. He grabbed my face and forced me to look into his eyes, informing me that he was 'beginning to like me too much' and he would be 'taking me for a drive' when he came home. In that moment I knew he was going to kill me that night," Alicia explains. *"Mommy, Daddy, please hurry!"* she prayed.

As the hours passed, Alicia began to see the cold, shallow grave waiting for her lifeless body. Silently she cried for her parents, although she knew it was unlikely she would see them again. As Alicia struggled to accept her impending death, she could not help but wonder if her parents knew how much she loved them.

"I didn't expect to get out of this alive. Any person who could kidnap and rape a child is likely capable of murder," Alicia says.

As she lay in the dark, hugging the abductor's kitten—its fur wet from her tears—she drifted into a dissociative state. Then, around four o'clock in the afternoon, she was suddenly jolted into a state of heightened awareness. The front door crashed loudly as it was knocked down by men yelling, "We've got guns!"

In her confused state, Alicia believed the captor had sent the men to kill her. Terrified, she crawled under the bed, dragging the heavy chain behind her. Men searched the house, making their way to the room, where Alicia lay hiding under the bed. Terrified, she tried to remain silent and hidden. Suddenly, Alicia heard a man's booming voice, "Movement…over there!"

As he walked towards the bed, Alicia could see only his boots; but the man's voice rang loud and clear when he commanded her to crawl out and put her hands up above her head.

Alicia crawled hesitantly from under the bed, as instructed. Trying to cover herself as she put her hands up, she was staring into the barrel of a gun.

"Then the man turned around to call the others, and I saw the three most beautiful letters in the alphabet written in bold yellow on his jacket: *FBI*," Alicia explains.

When the agents rescued Alicia they found a horrific sight. The girl was bruised, starved, and chained naked to the floor.

"The officers cut the chain from around my neck and set me free. I was given a second chance at life. One of the agents immediately took off his coat to cover my body," Alicia says. The agent's gesture convinced her that she was finally safe.

The internet predator, thirty-eight-year-old Scott Tyree, was a computer programmer. Today, Alicia never mentions him by name, instead referring to him only by terms such as "the offender".

Years earlier, the abductor had moved from California to Herndon, Virginia. He had divorced his wife, with whom he had a daughter. The daughter often visited her dad for holidays, and on that New Year's Day, he dropped his then twelve-year-old daughter off at the airport before driving approximately 250 miles to Pittsburgh to abduct Alicia.

According to Pittsburgh media, Scott Tyree's ex-wife described the father's and daughter's relationship as one of "kindred spirits"; they collected comic books and played computer games together. But when members of law enforcement searched Scott Tyree's computer they discovered he was anything but a loving father. The investigation revealed a sadomasochist who dreamed of becoming the master of teenage sex slaves. For nine months he had trolled internet chat rooms to find a suitable victim. Before he drove to Pittsburgh, he messaged an online acquaintance, writing: "I got one in Pittsburgh. I am going to get her. Handcuffs ready."

This was, however, not enough for Scott Tyree. He wanted to boast of his conquest and felt that he was living his fantasy. In order to do this, he livestreamed videos of himself torturing her. The predator shared the videos in an online forum with his "like-minded friends", who also fantasised of dominating and abusing young girls. One such viewer, a man in Tampa, Florida, had been surfing the same forums as Scott Tyree. He recognised the tortured girl in the video as someone he had recently seen in news stories and on "missing person" flyers. The viewer used a payphone to anonymously contact the FBI. The man told the investigators what he had been watching online, and he revealed one very important piece of information, namely, one of the perpetrator's online usernames: *masterforteenslavegirls*.

"An online acquaintance of the offender most likely reported the crime, as he feared he might be considered an accomplice," Alicia observes.

With the help of Yahoo!, law enforcement specialists were able to track Scott Tyree through his IP address. They immediately raided his home—minutes, even seconds, count when trying to rescue a child who has been abducted. Those minutes can determine whether a child survives a violent sexual offender once his fantasy has become a reality.

While agents rescued Alicia from the house of horror, other law enforcement officers arrested Scott Tyree as he was preparing to leave work and go home to take Alicia for what would probably have been her last drive.

"It is a miracle I am here today. I was very lucky," Alicia says.

When she went missing, law enforcement officers told her parents that the odds of finding their daughter were a million to one. Alicia, though, was the exception, and when she returned to her parents' house, media from all over the country congregated outside. Everyone wanted to hear the miraculous story of the child's unexpected rescue.

"I am very, very happy and very relieved," then thirteen-year-old Alicia, dazed and traumatised, answered when reporters asked how she felt to be reunited with her parents.

Not everyone saw Alicia's recovery as simply a happy story. Some members of the public started questioning why a thirteen-year-old girl had been chatting with a much older man. Alicia says that even today, critics incorrectly claim that her abduction might have been avoided if her parents had better supervised their daughter's chats and used a computer monitoring program to track her online activity. According to Alicia, this response arises from ignorance of what online "grooming" was like during the early years of the internet.

"This was the introductory period of internet usage, and parents were unaware of internet dangers," Alicia explains. "There was simply no internet safety education and little information concerning monitoring software available at that time."

A HAPPY CHILD

When Alicia entered the new millennium, she also entered an online world that was unknown to many people. Only half of all Americans were using the internet at that time, and most of them were young people who "adopted" the new technology faster than adults.

"Our parents grew up making friends at school or while playing in their neighbourhoods, but my generation did not only make friends in this way. We also made them online. Parents thought their children were safe, because they were at home and not roaming the streets," Alicia explains.

It was also difficult for adults to understand that a computer might represent a danger to children, because, after all, the screen was often right there in the family room for everyone to see.

"And back then, there were no stories of online predators," Alicia notes. "Grooming of children through the internet was a new threat that had not yet been addressed widely. It was more of an urban legend. Parents did not know how dangerous this new technology could be," she explains.

Ignorant of the manner in which a child might be groomed, some people suggest that when a thirteen-year-old girl voluntarily meets a stranger—a stranger whom she first met online—the encounter must have come about as the result of a broken or unhappy home.

"But nothing could be further from the truth in my case," Alicia says.

Her mother was a stay-at-home mom, devoted to her family and involved in the community. She was always highly supportive of her daughter. She volunteered for her daughter's field trips and was always available to bake cookies or help with homework. On the other hand, her father was a businessman who worked long hours from Monday through Saturday.

"I missed him, but then Sunday came and we would always go on family trips together with my brother, Chuck, who is nine years old[er] than me," Alicia fondly recalls. "We would go boating and spend time together as a family. I loved those Sundays. My parents are amazing people and I have always felt very fortunate and loved," Alicia explains, trying to eliminate misconceptions that suggest young girls who are lured by online predators are wild children searching for love through the internet because they cannot find it at home.

"Any child can become the victim of an internet predator. It's about vulnerability—and every child is vulnerable. Child sexual abuse and exploitation does not discriminate based on circumstance, background, or socioeconomic status," Alicia says.

When she recalls her background and upbringing she quickly describes it as being like a happy scene from a Disney movie. Though she knew there was evil in the world it was just so far away.

"As a small child, I would walk around singing out of joy. I was probably a bit naive [about] the real world," she acknowledges, "but at the same time I was just a happy kid enjoying my life. Later, I was so sad to find out that life is not like a musical where everybody dances and sings."

Recently Alicia had old home movies transferred onto digital media. Watching the movie clips was a trip down memory lane that brought back glimpses of the many joyful, childish moments she experienced. But the clips also showed who Alicia once was…and never will be again.

In one of the movies, Alicia sits in front of a Christmas tree. The beads in her hair gleam under the light of the Christmas ornaments. While unwrapping presents, she laughs and smells the new perfume she had hoped for. A few days later her childish laughter ceased when she was taken and forever changed.

"I miss that happy child. That child was murdered in the dungeon," Alicia says.

After the abduction, Alicia suffered from post-traumatic stress disorder (PTSD) and the resulting memory loss. Today, she does not remember many details from the actual kidnapping. But, she does remember how computers entered her life.

At home, Alicia watched with curiosity as her older brother used the computer. Her sibling often played online games, and Alicia realised she could do the same.

"It was great because you did not have to ask your parents if a friend could come over and play a game, the friends were already right there," Alicia says.

Like many children, Alicia spent a lot of time online, not only playing games, but also conducting research. She was highly interested in history, and she loved the information available online about the Holocaust, the attack on Pearl Harbor, and other historical events. She enjoyed taking her studies beyond what she learned in the classroom.

"My parents thought they had given their children a wonderful gift which we could use for both fun and schoolwork," Alicia explains.

The daughter was grateful for the gift. Although Alicia was a happy child she was also shy. There were times she would not raise her hand in class even if she knew the answer to the teacher's question. But, in front of the computer screen, she felt comfortable.

Online, she didn't have to compete in popularity contests with other girls, which was a relief. Puberty, of course, can be a time of struggle for young girls as they wrestle with their self-esteem. And so it was for Alicia. But when she logged on to the internet, all insecurities disappeared, and she felt free to ask all sorts of questions without being embarrassed.

"As a shy child, this was a place I could express myself freely. Most importantly, I felt safe. I was in my home, the safest place in the world," Alicia says.

She describes the internet as her generation's clubhouse. This clubhouse contained various "chat rooms" where strangers would happily talk with each other. And the children always got along with each other—unlike in a physical clubhouse. Or, as Alicia explains, the online universe was in many ways unexplored…and back then it seemed that no one had heard of cyberbullying.

"My parents had talked to me about 'stranger danger', but that does not translate well to the online world," Alicia says. "Everyone is a stranger before you meet them and get to know them. Online, you feel as though you know someone quickly. There were no discussions at that time about the dangers of meeting someone online. There were no other horror stories to warn children or their parents. I was also, as many children are, naive. I thought, because I was honest online, others were too. That's the thing, when you are young, you believe, and want to believe that the world, and the people in it, are good. It is part of innocence. An innocence I soon lost."

THE BOOGEYMAN

Alicia often met the same people "virtually" when she entered the chatrooms. One of them was "Christeen". For months Alicia chatted with the supposedly beautiful, red-haired, fourteen-year-old girl about the sorts of topics that come to mind when you are a teenager experiencing puberty.

"I shared all my thoughts and intimate secrets with her, and she always made me feel like she understood me. We were there for each other, and she became a close friend," Alicia shares.

After months of chatting online there was little about Alicia, her parents, and her life in general that Christeen didn't know. When the girls didn't share secrets they traded school pictures.

Alicia had no reason to believe that Christeen was not an honest teenager like herself. Christeen even had the same interest in music and clothes as Alicia, and she used the same teenage slang.

"But Christeen turned out to be a middle-aged man, named John. Everything he said was a lie. 'Christeen' was not real," Alicia observes. "It is clear that he, as online groomers do, studied children and knew exactly what to say to make me believe that he was a young girl. He had a lot of practice with his masquerade," Alicia notes.

John was not the only one playing a role in the masquerade. His friend, Scott Tyree, also shared the same twisted sexual interest in minors; both men knew how to play games with innocent children. While Alicia was still under the impression that Christeen was her peer, she was introduced to Scott Tyree.

"These predators chat online, where they brag to each other about their conquests and pass their 'little girlfriends' around to each other. I was one of them," Alicia says.

Alicia chatted with Scott Tyree for nine months, not knowing his true intentions and identity. So, she started trusting him. He always seemed to be online when she logged on, and if Alicia had a question, he would have the perfect answer and friendly advice.

"He was my confidant…he was interested in me and my life," Alicia recalls. "Most importantly, and [this was] effective in the grooming process, he was always on my side. He told me what I wanted to hear."

When it comes to online grooming, the predator's first step is gaining the trust of the child. The second step is sparking the child's natural curiosity about sex.

"[My abductor] started slowly introducing things of a sexual nature and led me into more intimate conversations. As a teenager, you have these natural curiosities. Also, he was my friend. I did not want to hurt his feelings or make him feel like I was not also willing to be there for him," Alicia notes.

Through the grooming process, Scott Tyree brainwashed Alicia. Slowly he pulled the girl away from her parents. When Alicia spoke about her parents, he would magnify and highlight the small arguments she had with her mother and father, twisting the minor disagreements until they started to feel like huge problems.

"The online predator's goal is to make the child feel like this relationship is the only thing that matters, and that this person is the only one who can truly understand you," Alicia observes. "This is what he did to me. He made me feel alone, although I was surrounded by love from my family."

Alicia needed to be rescued—but nobody knew it yet. Not even her family. Today, Alicia says, Scott Tyree effectively separated her from her parents, the very people who would have done anything to keep that from happening to their daughter.

"Groomers often build a wall between you and the people who love you. Then they take you apart so they can put you back together bit by bit, in a way that you are still you, yet somehow not. The problem is, the child does not realise that it is happening. It's subtle. Eventually, you may feel an obligation to return their attention and friendship. You feel you owe it to them," Alicia says.

And Scott Tyree was successful in both dismantling and reconstructing Alicia. In the end, she would do almost anything he asked her to do. Therefore, today she also feels that it was not Alicia opening the front door on New Year's Day. Rather, it was a thirteen-year-old girl who had been manipulated to do so.

"I was afraid of the dark and I rarely went outside on my own, much less at night. Yet I walked out to meet a complete stranger. Everything about that moment was out of my character," she recalls, "but I felt I had no other choice than to walk out that door."

Alicia says that at the end of her parents' driveway that night she found out that the boogeyman is real, that he lives on the internet, and that meeting him in real life can prove fatal. Today, Alicia works to keep other children safe, finding a purpose to pursue as a result of surviving her nightmare. Therefore she has a message to all parents:

"It sounds a bit juvenile, but the boogeyman does exist. Right now, somewhere not far from you, possibly in your own home, a predator is talking to a child online. He is grooming this child, gaining the child's trust only to betray them in the most vile way. This is what happened to me, and it can happen to your children. It has happened many times before. There are many stories we will never hear, because these children did not survive, are still missing, or otherwise silenced."

Alicia also says that she has a message for children:

"We often think that horrible things happen to other people, until it happens to you, or someone you know. Let me be that person that you know: I was a kid, just like you. If it can happen to me, it can happen to you. That's why you have to protect yourself. That's why you have to be careful. The threat is real. You must be aware of the dangers in order to use the tools to protect yourself. Your parents, teachers, loved ones, can do everything in their power to keep you safe, but when it comes down to it, you are the one who has the power to end that conversation, tell a trusted adult, and not walk out of that door," Alicia says.

To prevent other children from experiencing the same torture she did, Alicia decided to found the organisation called The Alicia Project, just one year after she was rescued.

THE PAIN RETURNS

Alicia first began sharing her story at the age of fourteen. She created The Alicia Project, because little to no internet safety education was being taught in schools. Alicia offered experience and expertise to other children as a means to empower them. She not only shared her story but also provided the tools to help children keep themselves safe and make healthy choices, both online and off. Alicia's goal has always been to save one child, one family, from what she experienced. She knows that to save one life is to change the world.

"I was able to take this horrible, awful event that happened to me and give it a purpose—and that purpose is to protect children," Alicia says today.

Alicia has done this successfully. Often, after her presentations, children ask to speak with her, to share what they have learned, as well as their own stories. Alicia recalls the time a student was grateful for her insights. The student talked about how she had been corresponding with a person online, sharing pictures, and was soon planning to meet him in person. After hearing Alicia's presentation, she recognised the red flags and decided to not take the risk.

Today, Alicia describes herself as a true pioneer and vision-ary for insightful internet safety and sexual exploitation awareness presentations to children and adults. As an advocate, she has testified before the US Congress to pass the federal Protect Our Children Act. Following that, she lobbied for passage of Alicia's Law, her namesake, in eleven states, alongside the National Association to Protect Children (PROTECT). Alicia's Law creates a dedicated revenue stream, funds the Internet Crimes Against Children (ICACs) network, and makes an indelible impact on how cases are investigated by assisting law enforcement. Tens of thousands of predators have been arrested since Alicia's Law passed. Recently, her heartfelt and passionate efforts were pointedly recognised when a K9 officer was named "Kozak"—a play on Alicia's family name. This police dog alerts agents to hidden flash drives, SD cards, and cell phones, sniffing out the chemical compound found in adhesives used in the devices.

"I won't stop until Alicia's Law has been passed in all fifty states," she says.

Less than two percent of known child exploitation cases are currently being investigated, due to a lack of dedicated federal resources, Alicia explains. However, Alicia's Law provides funding to the ICAC task force, enabling them to rescue endangered children.

When Alicia testified before Congress when she was just nineteen years old, she said:

"I was blessed by the simple fact that I live in Pittsburgh, where one of the very best cyber-crime task forces was created, and because I was enslaved in Virginia, where one of the best Internet Crimes Against Children task forces, or ICAC, exists. Because they had the training, the knowledge and the expertise to find that needle in the haystack, because they were there, I am here," Alicia explained.

Alicia says that Alicia's Law makes it possible for state and local agencies to obtain funding from various sources. Alicia and the National Association to Protect Children work with each state's government to design the best methods for appropriate funding. The funds can come from unclaimed lotteries and finances accumulated from misdemeanor and felony convictions, which means the money does not always have to come from a budget but from other dedicated sources. Among other things, the money funds the training of task forces' and agencies' efforts to find children who have become victims of sexual exploitation.

"Alicia's Law funds the boots on the ground, the actual law enforcement officers, who go out and save real children who are in danger," Alicia says.

Alicia also works in other ways to help prevent young girls and boys from suffering abduction, sexual abuse, and exploitation. In 2016, she graduated from The Chicago School of Professional Psychology with a master's degree in forensic psychology in order to understand victimology and predator behaviour from an academic perspective, in addition to understanding it from her own experience.

Alicia is also an Airline Ambassadors International Human Trafficking Awareness trainer. In her role as a trainer, she teaches airline personnel ways in which they can identify and report victims of human trafficking.

"By sharing my story I want to provide hope for others, because there is always hope, and hope is one thing that can never be taken from us," Alicia explains.

The road to helping other victims and preventing predatory crimes has been extremely rewarding and cathartic for Alicia; but there are days that prove to be harder than others, she observes. Though her victimisation has ended, the residual pain can continue in various forms. Flashbacks, PTSD, and nightmares are a reality. Unexpected triggers, she says, can sneak up on you.

"There are times when I do still experience triggers; however, over the years, you learn coping mechanisms [for] how best to manage them."

Following traumatic sexual abuse, romantic relationships can also prove difficult for the victim. Therefore, it is important to find a partner who has a high level of understanding and the emotional awareness to accept that there may be instances when victims require an absence of physical contact, while there may be other moments when they need closeness and comfort.

"As it pertains to trust, you must first learn to trust yourself and in your ability to make good decisions. Then you must begin to trust your environment and the world, and to believe that it is not simply filled with those who intend to do you harm. Finally, you have to trust a significant other enough to let them in to your private space and personal world. It took many years before I understood that rape is about power and control. Love never is," Alicia says. She shares that while visiting New York City, she met the man who won her trust and her heart. The couple married in 2016.

Alicia's transformation from victim to survivor has also required making choices other than trusting a partner.

A few years ago, Alicia traveled back to the house of evil in Virginia, where it had felt as if she had spent a lifetime before being freed. Jim Moore, the detective who escorted Alicia out of the house when she was rescued, accompanied her. When they arrived at the house Alicia first dared to look through the windows into the basement. Windows that had once been painted black to hide the room of torture. The room was now a child's sunny playroom. For Alicia, it was a sad yet peace-filled moment. Although the house had moved on—it was now a place of childhood joy—Alicia could not help but feel that parts of her remain forever trapped there.

"I cried inside for the child that I was who will forever be trapped there, but the woman I have become will remain strong and continue to be a voice for those victims still suffering," Alicia says.

There is also another part of Alicia's life she will never be able to erase. Scott Tyree will forever be an unwanted part of her history. And recently he has once again become a very present part of Alicia's life.

FACE TO FACE AGAIN

In 2002 Senior U.S. District Court Judge William Standish sentenced Scott Tyree to almost twenty years in prison for the abduction of Alicia, and for inflicting serious bodily injury, restraining the victim, exploiting the girl's vulnerability, and victimising a thirteen-year-old girl. The sentence was the result of a plea bargain.

In early 2019, a reporter contacted Alicia and asked if she was aware that Scott Tyree had been released from the federal prison in North Carolina before serving his full sentence. Furthermore, the reporter noted, Scott Tyree had been transferred to a halfway house just four miles from where he abducted Alicia—and where her family still lives. Alicia immediately panicked.

"I just let out an anguished scream and dropped my phone," Alicia explains today.

The moment she received the news that her abductor had been released into her community, Alicia's world fell apart. She started to fear for both her life and the lives of her parents. And she will forever remember how her mother reacted when Alicia called to convey the message that the abductor was now living a short drive from her parents' homes.

"My mother's scream will haunt me forever. I heard and felt her terror," Alicia says.

When Scott Tyree decided to move to Pittsburgh—a city where he still remains as of the writing of this book, and a city where he previously had no family, friends, or ties of any kind—he also made another choice, Alicia says.

"He may have come to finish what he started. I feel that my family and I are in immediate danger," she explains.

Not only does Alicia feel terrified, she also feels betrayed by a system that makes it possible for an offender to request that he be released into the community where he was prosecuted, even though he has no connection to the place.

The decision to move Scott Tyree to a location near his victim sparked an outrage among several members of Congress. They demanded that the Bureau of Prisons relocate him, but the authorities refused, stating that they installed the kidnapper in the halfway house in Pittsburgh to facilitate his reintegration into the community.

"Beyond the fact that he had been released into my parents' community," Alicia notes, "I was shocked to find out that there was no GPS ankle-monitoring of him, and there were no restrictions preventing him from showing up at my parents' house. It shows that in America offenders may have more rights than the victims."

After petitioning the court for heightened protections from her abductor, Alicia's lawyers successfully garnered a court order forcing Scott Tyree to wear a GPS ankle monitor. However, the court order was valid for a period of only six months. Alicia is now engaged in a legal battle with the government in order to get the perpetrator moved out of Pittsburgh. And she has asked to be allowed to testify in court at the relocation hearing.

Alicia says she wants to make her voice heard in court in the same way that her voice has been heard numerous times as a victim's advocate at public events. Over the years, Alicia has spoken to hundreds of thousands of students around the world. The students often ask her if she still viewed the man who abducted her as a threat. Before Scott Tyree's release from prison, Alicia answered that he no longer mattered, because he was in prison, and her focus had been on the predators who are still out there. Today she can no longer give that answer.

"Since he was released I have experienced nearly every emotion. I have cried, I have been numb, I have felt powerless and I have been enraged. I again fear for my life, because this man has clearly shown that he has no problem inflicting emotional and psychological harm," Alicia observes.

And those sorts of emotions know no boundaries. Recently, Alicia moved to New York City. When she did, she made a promise to herself and to her family that she would come back to Pittsburgh to visit her parents at least once a month. However, this promise will not be possible for her to fulfill, because as long as Scott Tyree is in Pittsburgh there can be no guarantee she will be safe, Alicia says. And her plans of one day moving back to her hometown have also been cancelled for as long as her perpetrator resides in the city.

"Pittsburgh has become a place of terror, his presence here has resulted in several panic attacks," she says.

Alicia experienced a panic attack when she was driving home to celebrate Easter with her family. She had been driving for more than six hours when she saw Pittsburgh outlined in the distance. It had always been a welcoming sight, but now seeing Pittsburgh looming up ahead causes Alicia only fear.

"I just grabbed my husband's hand and started crying," Alicia says of her Easter experience.

The offender's release has brought back other memories. Alicia recalls how, as an older child, she at times feared that her abductor would escape prison and come haunt her, but her mother would comfort her by explaining the difference between anxiety and fear.

"*Anxiety* is when there is a tiger in a cage at the zoo, and you are scared it will break loose and get you. *Fear* is that same tiger loosed and in your neighbourhood," Alicia explains. "Today he is loose in my neighbourhood again."

When she asked permission to speak at the hearing regarding whether authorities should force Scott Tyree to leave Pittsburgh, Alicia says she did it not only for her own sake, but also for the sake of those victims who currently live their own lives in fear resulting from the same circumstances. Setting a legal precedent in this case will help to ensure that future victims and survivors will not have to suffer as Alicia and other victims are suffering right now.

"The offender wants a victim that does not speak up. But I have not been that victim," Alicia says. "I stood up against him, against all predators, for all these years, and I have loudly spoken out. I have fought for nearly twenty years, and I will never stop fighting to end predatory crimes against children. My voice will never be silenced, and I will fight to raise theirs."

Continuing her fight while simultaneously taking it to the next level, Alicia has recently joined the International Centre for Missing & Exploited Children (ICMEC), where she is currently the director of Outreach and Global Impact. The centre's combined mission is to "unite the world in the prevention, response, recovery, and healing of every missing, abused, and exploited child to make certain that no matter where they are or how they got there, no child stands alone."

ICMEC collaborates with every industry—from government to technology, from sports to entertainment—through six programs dedicated to the advancement of every country's child protection capabilities. ICMEC has partnered with law enforcement in India to launch their first cyber child sexual exploitation unit. The centre has also partnered with giants in the technology industry to launch the Global Missing Children's Network's "GMCNgine," which uses artificial intelligence, geo-targeting, and facial recognition software to search both the dark and clear web to help find missing and exploited children. Alicia moderated a panel with the GMCNgine's creators at the 2019 SXSW (South by Southwest) Conference.

Paul Shapiro, ICMEC's president and CEO, and a fellow Pittsburgher, shares the centre's vision of defending the rights of children on a global scale. Combining the international centre's programs with Alicia's expertise and passion creates the launching point where policymakers, education and medical professionals, law enforcement agencies, technology companies, and partner organisations can all unite to bring an end to child abduction, sexual abuse, and exploitation.

"We have to unite," Alicia asserts. "We have to stand together to face this epidemic, because it is not a political issue, a demographic issue, an economic issue, or a geographic issue. The future and safety of our children is a human issue," she says.

2

TAKEN BY A STRANGER

Stranger abductions are the rarest form of abductions, but they are normally the ones that make headlines as they are most likely to have a fatal outcome.

Every year approximately 115 American children are taken by a complete stranger or someone who is only a slight acquaintance of the child. A former study from the US Department of Justice showed that four out of ten children taken by a stranger never made it home alive. Today, however, experts estimate that more children are recovered due to technological advances and well-organised alert programs such as AMBER, which help law enforcement to track and solve the crimes.

A stanger abduction typically happens when a child is travelling to or from school or school-related activities. These abductions most often take place within a quarter mile of the child's home, while the victim is playing, walking, or riding a bike in the street. Roughly eight out of ten victims are girls between the age of twelve and seventeen years.

When a child successfully evades an attempted stranger abduction it is typically because the child ignores the abductor in the first place, uses their cell phone to threaten intervention, fights back, screams, or is saved by an adult's intervention.

Based on the analysis of almost 10,000 attempted abductions, the National Center for Missing and Exploited Children has concluded that the five most common lures are:

- *Offering the child a ride (28 percent of attempted stranger abductions)*

- *Asking the child questions (18 percent of attempted stranger abductions)*

- *Offering the child candy or other sweets (11 percent of stranger abductions)*

- *Offering the child money (8 percent of stranger abductions)*

- *Showing an animal to the child to gain their attention (7 percent of stranger abductions)*

Erin Runnion's five-year-old daughter, **Samantha,** was taken by a stranger. When the mother gave her victim impact statement in court on the day Samantha's abductor was sentenced to death, she tearfully addressed the killer sitting only a few feet away:

"You don't deserve a place in my family's history. And so I want you to live. I want you to disappear into the abyss of a lifetime in prison where no one will remember you, no one will pray for you, and no one will care when you die."

A BRAVE GIRL!

Missing: Samantha Bree Runnion
Date of Birth: 07/26/1996
Missing From: Stanton, California
Date of Crime: 07/15/2002 (5 years old)
Classification: Endangered Missing
Interview: Erin Runnion, mother of Samantha

Samantha loved the blossom season, and she gladly helped her mother arrange the flower bed outside the condo where her family lived. That day they filled the earth with sunflowers, which Samantha could hardly wait to see bloom. Unfortunately she never would. Shortly after Samantha helped seed life, her own life was taken.

Around six thirty P.M. on that hot summer night, five-year-old Samantha was playing with her friend, Sarah, outside of the Smoketree condominium complex in Stanton, where she lived. While playing, the girls observed a man who passed them by, driving a green car. The man drove around the block before coming back a second time. This time he pulled up near the girls, parked his vehicle, and approached the two children, asking if they would help him find his chihuahua. Samantha, who cared for animals, kindly asked how big the dog was, but the man suddenly grabbed her and threw the child into his car while the little girl kicked and screamed for help.

"Go tell my Grandma!" Samantha cried.

Sarah quickly ran to tell the grandmother, who was babysitting the children.

When the police arrived, Sarah, who was one year older than Samantha, gave the detectives a detailed description of the young Hispanic man with the slick, black hair and thin mustache who had forced Samantha into his car.

Sarah's description was so detailed that when a police sketch of the suspect was released, the police received several calls from prospective witnesses, who all identified the same man. But Samantha's body was found the day after her abduction, before the man was arrested.

"Oh my God, we found a dead body," a man's frantic voice exclaimed to the 911 operator he had called. "Please hurry. I'm so scared. It's a little kid." He had made the discovery while hiking a mountain trail in Cleveland National Forest, more than fifty miles south of Samantha's home.

One life had been taken, but another life was just sprouting.

"The morning after she was found," her mother explains, "there was suddenly a sunflower in full bloom. It was red, which was Samantha's favourite colour, despite [the fact that] we had only planted yellow sunflowers. I believe it was like Samantha's way of giving me a kiss goodbye."

When police officers arrived at the scene where the body was found they were met by a horrific sight. The girl was naked and had been positioned in such a way that detectives believed the murderer had seen his kill as some kind of a trophy. As if he was showing off his "work".

"The fact it was not buried, not hidden, it was almost like a calling card: 'I'm here and I'm going to strike again," Richard Garcia, the agent in charge of the FBI's violent crime unit in Los Angeles, said.

Law enforcement immediately launched a manhunt. More than two hundred officers searched for the killer, and dozens of FBI agents were assigned to assist local cops on instructions of President George W. Bush, who expressed his sympathy for the Runnion family. The case became breaking news all over America.

"The kidnapping or murder of a child is every parent's worst nightmare," Bush said at a ceremony shortly after Samantha was taken. Directly referencing not only Samantha but also other children who had become victims of evil perpetrated by adults during the summer of 2002, the president continued: "Our nation has come to know the names and faces of too many wonderful children, because they've been the victims of despicable violence."

Erin experienced the support from more than simply the nation's president. People were so touched by the malicious murder of an innocent child that more than 4,000 people attended Samantha's funeral when Erin buried her daughter.

Not far from the crime scene, in Lake Elsinore, another mother followed the media's coverage of the news. While watching television, she told her son that she hoped law enforcement would catch the killer soon. Her son replied by asking his mother whether she wished the murderer would be sentenced to death. Her reply was: "Yes." Five days later her son, Alejandro Avila, was arrested.

The twenty-seven-year-old man worked as a production line supervisor at a medical equipment plant. He matched the description of the perpetrator. Phone records later showed that he had been in the area where Samantha lived at around the time she was taken. His credit card records revealed he had rented a room at a Comfort Inn in Temecula, near the road that led to the trail where Samantha was found. Alejandro Avila checked in sometime shortly after nine P.M. on the day Samantha went missing. Detectives suspected the Comfort Inn was where he molested and killed the child.

To determine Alejandro Avila's whereabouts and the timeline for the crime, investigators drove the route from the Smoketree complex to the Comfort Inn. The investigators started out from Samantha's home at 6:17 P.M. and, after stopping at the service stations where, through the perpetrator's bank statements, they had learned the suspect had also stopped, they arrived at the Comfort Inn. The time was 8:57 P.M. Law enforcement searched Alejandro Avila's car, a 1994 Ford Thunderbird, which eventually left no doubt. Droplets of a clear liquid were seeping in to the material inside the suspect's vehicle.

"Samantha had been crying," Erin Runnion explains, "and the DNA evidence came from her tear drops."

A FIGHTER

While investigating the crime police also discovered Alejandro Avila's DNA under Samantha's nails. Although Samantha weighed only forty-two pounds and her killer's weight was over two hundred pounds, she had still been fighting for her life up to the final moments, scratching Alejandro Avila till he bled. Even as Samantha took her last breath she lived up to her favourite motto: "Be brave".

"He had a huge cut on the back of his leg and arm. I am so proud that Samantha had the courage to fight him," Erin says.

Not that it surprised Erin. She has many beautiful memories of her daughter, whom she describes as a remarkable child who, at an early stage in life, showed that she wanted to make the most of it.

"She was a fighter right from her birth," Erin recalls. "Like a turtle coming out of the shell she lifted her head to look at me, just three days old; and when she was five months old a group of friends came to see her. While they were here Samantha was turning pages in a book. And Samantha was just ten months old when she started walking. She was pretty remarkable. I believe that somehow she knew that she only had a short time here with us, which gave her the drive to make the most of her time."

The mother also remembers every minute of the day her daughter was taken. Erin could not just sit around the house waiting for news, so she started searching for Samantha herself. Together, with her fiancé, Kenneth, she drove around the neighbourhood, where they put up posters with Samantha's beautiful, smiling face. Erin had gone into search mode and would not stop till her daughter was found. But suddenly, by the end of the evening, she felt paralysed.

"I got this flash of Samantha going through my body crying: 'Mama!'. I just felt like grabbing her. But I knew at that moment that she was probably dead, and it was also later determined that she was killed around the same time I had that flash," Erin says.

The mother describes how everything became very foggy when her daughter was found the next day, and she realised that Samantha was never coming back.

The meaningless murder of a little girl raised so many questions for Erin about what had happened and why. However, Erin did not have to wait long before she would be able to put a face on the man who had taken her daughter. After the police sketch of the suspect was released, police quickly received the first tips suggesting they investigate Alejandro Avila. This was not the first time the investigators' attention was drawn to this particular suspect.

One year before Samantha was killed, Alejandro Avila had been charged with lewd and lascivious conduct perpetrated against two six-year-old girls. One of the girls was the daughter of the suspect's ex-girlfriend, with whom he had recently split up. But when the case went to trial, Alejandro Avila was acquitted of all charges. His lawyers stated that the girls lied and that the allegation against him had been fabricated because his ex-girlfriend was mad at him and wanted revenge.

Although Alejandro Avila was acquitted of the lascivious conduct charges, this case showed that he was familiar with the area around

Samantha Runnion's home, if not with Samantha herself, as his ex-girlfriend lived in the same complex as the Runnion family.

The suspect himself now lived with his sister, Elvira, in an apartment on Riverside Drive in Lake Elsinore. His mother and a second sister also lived in the same complex. On the day Samantha was taken, Alejandro Avila had promised to cook dinner for the family; it was expected to be ready at six P.M. But he never came home to cook the meal, and when detectives interrogated him he could not account for his whereabouts on the afternoon and evening when Samantha was killed. And when the defendant's sister, Elvira, was questioned, she told police that her brother was familiar with the area where Samantha was found: The sister had once gone there with Alejandro Avila to watch a meteor shower. She also said that the day after Samantha's disappearance she had noticed a scratch on the inside of her brother's knee. When she asked what had happened, the brother told her that he had scratched his knee on a baby gate while at the beach.

Five days after the crime was committed Sheriff Michael Carona of Orange County informed the public that law enforcement had made an arrest. Without hesitation he said law enforcement was "one hundred percent certain" that Alejandro Avila killed Samantha, and he sent a direct message to the killer:

"I told you we would hunt you down. If you thought for one minute we were kidding, tonight you know we were deadly serious."

Three years later, Alejandro Avila would know exactly what "dead serious" meant. When his trial started in 2005 the prosecutor asked that the defendant be sentenced to death.

The trial lasted five weeks. Erin was present in court every day. During the entire trial Alejandro Avila kept his head down and never once looked at the people gathered in the courtroom.

"I had waited and prepared three years for the trial, but going there was so surreal," Erin recalls. "There were so many things I did not understand. It was so hard accepting that a person could do this to a small child, and I went to the trial because I wanted to know every little detail of what had happened to Samantha so that I could stop imagining every possible horror," she says.

The mother also states that listening to what her daughter went through was devastating. An autopsy revealed that Samantha had been sexually assaulted, and that the little girl had suffered at least two blows to the head, which caused her brain to swell. The coroner also attested that so much blood exited from the head wound that Samantha likely drifted in and out of consciousness for several hours before her death.

"It was so tough listening to," Erin says, "but I wanted to know when and how [this murderer] hit her in the head. I just wanted to know as much as possible, so I could put the picture together. And I said to myself, that if Samantha could go through this being the victim, I could also go through listening to it."

The trial also provided Erin an explanation for why Alejandro Avila had abducted and killed her daughter.

NO REMORSE

The defence attorney used testimonies from Alejandro Avila's relatives to reveal that the man on trial came from a family that had been impoverished; sexually, physically, and psychologically abusive; and dysfunctional for generations.

The defendant's father had been arrested for child abuse; the children were then removed from the family home. A relative also testified that when they had been children, Alejandro Avila and his siblings had been locked up in a room where they were beaten repeatedly by the father, who would later be incarcerated for having murdered a neighbour.

Testimony at the trial also described how Alejandro Avila had lost two brothers. Both were killed in gang-related incidents. Today, Erin accepts that extremely harsh circumstances led Avila to become a monster.

"He had an unimaginable upbringing," Erin acknowledges. "When he was five years old an aunt walked in on his uncle raping him at a family party. It made sense he was capable of doing what he did, but that does not excuse his actions. He preyed on a tiny person to feel powerful. I will never really understand how a person can do such evil to a child even though he had experienced evil himself. I do feel sorry for the childhood he had, but I cannot forgive the twenty-seven-year-old person who murdered my daughter," Erin says.

During the trial, Deputy District Attorney Brent also revealed that police had found child pornography on Avila's computer. He stated that Avila was a paedophile who killed Samantha so as not to leave any evidence that he had sexually abused her, because he did not want to risk having to go through a trial like the one he had gone through when charged with molesting the two six-year-old girls. During the earlier trial involving the two girls, the jury had believed his testimony over that of the children. When Erin was a guest on *Larry King Live* on CNN just two months after Samantha's death, she said: "I blame every juror who let him go, every juror who sat on that trial and believed this man over those little girls."

Erin also blames Alejandro Avila for never having admitted he killed her daughter, and for not showing any remorse before, during, or after the trial. When Erin gave her victim impact statement in court, Alejandro Avila even turned away from her.

Erin says it is not up to her to forgive him for what he did; only Samantha has that right.

"Forgiveness is a difficult process. It is a topic I like to think and talk about because people always ask if I have forgiven him, but the act is unforgivable, and therefore it becomes difficult. I can understand and accept the truth of it, but the only one who can forgive him is Samantha," Erin says. "I know that if you don't forgive, you end up with anger that punishes you more than the person you are angry with. That is a motivation to forgive, and anger is not a natural part of me. Still, I am not the one to forgive him."

Although she cannot forgive Avila she often talks about him. Never by his name—because Erin believes he does not deserve to be recognised in that way, just as he does not deserve to be sensationalised by the media. Therefore, Erin feels disgusted when she sees Samantha's photo displayed next to Avila's in newspapers and other media.

"Murderers and victims are almost always pictured side by side, as if they were a couple," Erin notes.

She also believes that in notorious criminal cases such as her daughter's abduction and murder, as time passes public conscience often seems to shift towards glorifying the criminals and forgetting the victims. Erin was reminded of this a few years ago, when a newspaper produced an online slide show of infamous killers on California's Death Row, including the monster that took her daughter Samantha. The slide show featured brief descriptions of the crime alongside a colour photograph of each killer. The victims were mentioned only by name, Erin notes.

Still, she thinks it is important to share both Samantha's story and the story of her killer. Doing so, she says, shows us what creates the monsters who are capable of killing innocent children.

"When a child is abused and exposed to violence from childhood they are often stuck in an environment they cannot escape later in life," Erin observes.

Although she has not forgiven Avila, understanding why he became this monster (as Erin calls him) has helped Erin to move on.

"I literally do not feel any anger towards him anymore. And I genuinely hope that by the time he dies, he is in a place where he understands what he did and feels remorseful. When we die justice comes for us one way or another," Erin says. She adds that the biggest transition for her occurred at the end of the trial.

"I said to my husband and mother that I felt lighter and a huge burden was lifted off me when he was convicted. A part of that burden was the anger leaving," Erin says.

After five weeks of testimony, Avila was sentenced to death. He was sent to San Quentin, north of San Francisco. Erin was not surprised that he would pay with his own life for the one he took.

"We met the DA just after his arrest, and the DA told me that he wanted the death penalty, and that he was not going to negotiate it. I did not fight his decision, but in general I am against the death penalty, and today I do not wish to see him dead. There is no benefit from him dying," Erin says.

However, she is sure there is a lot to learn from Avila's upbringing and Samantha's death. Knowing details about Avila's childhood made Erin focus on both victims and perpetrators during the time that followed her daughter's death, because she did not want Samantha to have died in vain. Therefore, Erin decided to set up The Joyful Child Foundation, which is dedicated to prevent crimes against children through programs that educate, empower, and unite families and communities.

"When Samantha was found I hoped she would be the last child abducted and killed," Erin says, "but eleven days later, on the morning of Samantha's sixth birthday, I heard about another little girl abducted and killed in Kansas. So I decided I had to fight for the children and to help prevent others from becoming a victim like Samantha," the mother explains.

WARNED WHILE SLEEPING

Erin says that losing a child is a grief like no other. For a long time after Samantha's murder she felt she was never going to come out on the other side.

"But when I established The Joyful Child Foundation," she says, "it gave me a reason and a purpose." She adds that she "wants to ensure that every child is exposed to personal safety education and opportunities to practice [what they have learned] in order to cultivate each child's instinctual response to recognize, avoid, and if necessary, physically resist and escape inappropriate behaviors or violence."

Erin believes that as a society we need to do much more to protect children, because they cannot protect themselves. But she notes that we are often afraid to talk with our children about the dangers of the world, and that we do not teach them how to protect themselves against these dangers.

"We must teach our children that it is okay to say 'stop', to run away, or to fight back. We must empower our children without scaring them," Erin says.

The foundation has developed workshops for parents and children called "Be Brave—Be Safe Empowerment Programs". The foundation also teaches these programs within elementary school curricula. And, according to Erin, the children love it.

"We practise both verbal and physical skills," Erin explains. "We teach them self-confidence through words, but we also teach them how to back up the words with physical skills, if they have to, in order to get away from danger. Because the children are alone, they need to be empowered to deal with difficult situations. There can not be an adult around all the time. Therefore, we try to give them an understanding about what they should be concerned about, and we teach them so they feel, they are allowed to protect themselves, and that they can protect themselves."

There is a second reason Erin intrinsically knew she had to start the foundation. In the months leading up to Samantha's disappearance, some members of Samantha's family received the same dreadful warning.

"My mum, me, and Samatha all had nightmares where Samantha was killed. On one occasion Samantha came into my room and said: 'What should I do if he gets me into his car?'. I had no answer for her. That is also why I started the foundation. I feel guilty about having had the premonition and not being able to give her an answer. Now, I want to provide that answer for other children," Erin says. As a result of her desire to help children, she now works as a full-time child safety advocate.

The nightmares were not the first warnings Erin had. When she was fourteen years old she also had a dream in which her grandfather, who was already dead when Erin was born, appeared in a dream, warning her that something bad was going to happen to Erin and her family when she became an adult.

"I woke up hysterical from the dream and told my mom. But back then it was just a dream," Erin notes. "Today, we know it turned out to be real. The universe warned us a couple of times about what was going to happen, but how was I to know it would come true?" Erin wonders.

Since Samantha's death, her family has had more pleasant experiences. Especially Erin's mother.

"A few days after Samantha's death my mother woke up in the middle of the night and saw Samantha dancing around in circles in her bedroom. It was Samantha's way of saying she was okay. I wish I would have had the same experience," Erin says.

However, Erin does not need dreams to remember what a happy, smiling child her daughter was, and how she always showed compassion for others. Erin feels that she honours that memory by telling Samantha's story through the foundation's programs.

"She deserved to be remembered for who she was," Erin observes. "It would be a disgrace to her [if she were] always being remembered in a sad way, and it helped me to find joy again, focusing on Samantha deserving a beautiful legacy," she says.

It has also been important for Erin to keep the public's focus on Samantha as the victim, rather than Avila being sensationalised as a child killer and death row inmate. And this is just one of the reasons why Erin does not want to meet with Avila while he is in prison.

"I can't imagine why I would want to sit down with him," Erin states candidly. "He was *so* adamant about denying his crime at the trial, and I believe he still is. So that would make it even more difficult to meet him. I want a full confession, and I would want to know exactly what happened. My imagination about what [Samantha] went through is worse than having him tell what he did, but till the day he is prepared to confess there is no point in meeting him," Erin says.

Instead she focuses on spending time with her other three children, her son and two daughters. Erin has always tried to make sure they don't grow up in the shadows of Samantha's death.

Right after Samantha's passing, Erin would sit with a photo of her daughter and do nothing more than just cry. But slowly she realised that her additional children deserved a happy childhood. That recognition helped Erin move forward.

"They were my motivation to find joy again and to learn how to live with my grief. I would share my memories about Samantha with them, but I would not put the grief on them. I did not want them to worry about me," she explains.

However, her children still were affected by their sister's murder. For good and for worse. Samantha had a sister who was ten years old when she went missing. The sister is autistic, and until Samantha's disappearance she had been a very quiet and introverted child. The sad events led to a huge shift in her personality.

"She started to reach out. It was the impact of the trauma. Before, she did not have any kind of understanding about how others felt, but losing her sister was a major shift. Now she reads other's feelings and she tries to connect. Today," Erin says, "she is a very caring person, and you would not think she is autistic, because she no longer has many of the typical traits."

SO MUCH VIOLENCE

Samantha's autistic sister adjusted in positive and productive ways to Samantha's death. Samantha's brother, on the other hand, was deeply and adversely affected by his sister's brutal fate. He had turned five years old a month before Samantha was killed. Erin observes that he suffered the most trauma from losing not only his sister, but also his best friend.

"He was terrified that the killer would come back and do the same to him. Shortly after [Samantha's death] we moved to another place to make him feel more safe. I really wish I had done more to help him, but at that time I was so full of grief," Erin observes. She relates how proud she is of all her children, and that they eventually all came through the traumas of Samantha's death.

Today, Samantha's brother is applying for law school, as he has always held justice close at heart. When Samantha's murderer was on trial and finally sentenced to death, he asked Erin why there had to be so much violence and what good killing Avila would do.

"I understand his question. Imprisonment makes sense," Erin acknowledges. "People who hurt others need a lifetime of imprisonment to understand the horror of what they have done to others, but not necessarily through death. We need to trust that there is something much bigger going on and that there is love behind it when we leave it in the hands of our Creator," Erin says. She admits that she sees Samantha's fate in a very spiritual way. When Samantha was taken, however, Erin would question her own faith. Today, she says, she has decided which beliefs to hold on to.

"I wanted to be able to go into death totally open to whatever may await me, but I don't believe I will necessarily meet Samantha again in death. I will not cling to that hope, because I think it is super important to be open to whatever the truth is in our death."

Her first step of letting go occurred when she went to see Samantha's body at the coroner's office. Erin recalls how Samantha was pumped full of unnatural chemicals and the staff had smeared a lot of makeup on Samantha to cover up the bruises she suffered during her abduction and subsequent assault. She did not look herself, Erin says.

"My mom took my hand and said 'you have to let her go now'. She wanted to make sure I moved on. It is easy to feel sorry for yourself and get stuck with that feeling. When she held my hand I realised that Samantha's death would not stop my life. I had to live on," Erin says.

Sometime after seeing Samantha at the coroner's office she had another realisation.

"How could I feel sorry for myself after knowing what pain Samatha went through when she lost her life? I was still alive and had a beautiful family. That realisation has given me strength to accept joy again," Erin says.

Not one day goes by when Erin does not think of Samantha. Often, Erin feels as if her daughter is still around, as though Samantha is there in spirit, reading her mother's feelings and thoughts. At times Erin also feels her physical presence.

"I know my baby is gone," she says. "But if I see someone who looks like her, I still look twice, even though she would be twenty-three years old today," Erin observes.

3

HUMAN TRAFFICKING

Human trafficking, also known as modern-day slavery, is a crime that involves compelling or coercing a person to provide labour or to engage in commercial sex acts. And human trafficking represents a great danger to many Americans today.

The number of trafficked individuals is extremely difficult to verify due to the industry's clandestine nature, but the Global Slavery Index estimates that more than 400,000 people are living in modern-day slavery across the United States. Eight out of ten victims are women, and almost one-third are children who are often forced into prostitution, child labour, domestic work, or even forced to have their own organs removed. Roughly sixty percent of all victims are sexually exploited. Victims are as young as eleven years old, bought and sold alongside adults.

Often, the victims are lured by a human trafficker they have met online. Too late they realise that their so-called friend or soul mate did not, in fact, love them or have any intention of being a genuine friend. The only interest they had was to exploit them by becoming their pimp—or by selling them to one.

Human trafficking is a growing industry. According to the United Nations, selling illicit drugs is believed to be the only criminal activity today that is larger than trafficking human beings. However, today human trafficking is probably the fastest growing business for criminal organisations, because criminals can sell drugs only once, whereas a person can be sold again and again....

The International Labor Organization (ILO) estimates that human traffickers already earn profits of roughly $150 billion a year worldwide. In 2016, Microsoft, Wells Fargo, Samsung, JP Morgan, and Apple had annual net profit of $136 billion *combined*.

Human trafficking has been reported in all fifty states in the United States. Many victims are brought into the United States from Central America, Eastern Europe, and Asia; nevertheless, experts believe most human trafficking victims come from local American communities. Often, the victims are youths who have run away from home, girls from foster homes, or people who are vulnerable because of disabilities, homelessness, or drug abuse. But the victims also include highly functioning girls and women who are abruptly abducted from American streets.

Cindy Young has not seen her daughter **Christina** for nine years. The young mother of one is believed to have been kidnapped by a human trafficking ring and forced into prostitution in Illinois, just a two-and-a-half-hour drive from her home.

A SLAVE OF MODERN TIMES

Missing: Christina Maxine Whittaker
Date of Birth: 3/28/1988
Missing From: Hannibal, Missouri
Missing Since: 11/13/2009 (21 years old)
Classification: Endangered Missing
Interview: Cindy Young, mother of Christina

Hannibal, Missouri, has always been known best as the hometown of the world famous author Mark Twain. Novels such as *The Adventures of Tom Sawyer* and *Adventures of Huckleberry Finn* are inspired by Twain's time in Hannibal. In 2009, however, fiction wasn't what best described the small town. Rather, it was hard-core facts concerning a young mother of a six-month-old infant who had gone missing.

That day, Christina had dressed up in a pink tank top under a white V-neck T-shirt. She also wore brand new Nike sneakers with pink stripes. Christina was celebrating a special occasion: her first night out since giving birth to her daughter, Alexandria.

As she enjoyed a few hours of "freedom" with friends, one shot of tequila turned into too many. Just before midnight, Christina was thrown out of Rookie's Sports Bar after she harassed other bar patrons. When she landed on Broadway not only was she drunk, she was also helpless.

Christina's best friend promised to drive her home, but she did not want to leave the party at the bar early simply because of Christina's bad behaviour. The twenty-one-year-old woman was now on her own.

Christina had a habit of calling her mother, Cindy, several times a day, but that night she could not call her for help. Cindy had travelled to Texas with her husband, Alex, who was a professional truck driver. And although they were supposed to make it back home to Missouri on the day Christina went missing, they never did. Alex's truck had broken down.

"The one time my daughter needed me the most in her life I wasn't there for her. I will carry that guilt in my heart forever," Cindy explains.

Therefore, Christina wandered around the streets of downtown Hannibal on her own, asking several different people for a ride home. Everyone rejected her request. And so Christina decided to enter another bar to ask for help. She was last seen when she came running out of the bar's back entrance, tears streaming down her face.

"I am not in doubt," Cindy states confidently. "She met the guys who took her in that bar. They must have said or done something that made her run off crying."

Cindy believes that her daughter did not get far before the same guys grabbed her and forced her to come with them. And Cindy has no doubt that her daughter became desperate: Christina's phone was later found on the ground, just a few blocks from the bar, and when the phone was examined it showed she had called seven different people several times asking for help. No one answered her calls.

"She was very intoxicated that night and she must have been an easy target for the persons who took her," Cindy explains.

The mother describes her daughter as a very vulnerable person. Christina was being treated for bipolar disorder and anxiety, and she was taking prescription medication. The psychiatric medication made her susceptible to manipulation, her mother says.

"Christina has always been 'child-like' and naïve, which has made her easy to prey on by others," Cindy says. She often uses the present tense when referring to Christina, as she believes that referring to her daughter in the past tense would convey the sense that she has given up all hope of finding her daughter alive.

Christina began taking the psychiatric medication when she was eighteen years old, but she did not like the effects of the medication, so she took it irregularly. Since she disappeared, she has almost surely not had access to her medicine.

Given Christina's mental condition, some people have speculated that she has committed suicide, or that she left town by choice. But Cindy says those scenarios are not feasible.

"She was depressive, but she would never leave her little baby. She loved Alexandria, and this [town] was where she wanted to be. She was very happy with her family and just looking for that lift to get back to it," Cindy explains.

After the disappearance police conducted ground and water searches to see if an accident had befallen Christina. Given that no one was able to find the slightest trace of Christina, however, the mother has no doubt that her daughter's disappearance was the result of foul play. She believes the abductors knew of Christina's existence and had already planned on taking her.

"She met the wrong persons with the wrong intentions," Cindy asserts. "That night was the perfect time and place for them to grab Christina because of the circumstances."

The mother feels confident she knows what happened to her daughter because shortly after Christina's disappearance the identity of the kidnappers was confirmed to her by people who are familiar with the alleged perpetrators. Those same people are simply too scared to inform on their associates by going to the police, for they fear becoming victims themselves.

"They are four people, all family-related. I have been told that they belong to a group who sell and run drugs from Hannibal. We know who they are, and investigators have unofficially told me that they are their prime suspects," Cindy notes, "but they have not been able to prove in a court of law that they took Christina."

Cindy also says that she knows Christina is still alive.

"We were always close in spirit—and I can just feel that she is alive. We have also had so many indicators that she is. Right from when she was abducted till today."

Two weeks after Christina went missing, police and the family received their first tip. An informant said that Christina had been taken to Peoria, Illinois.

After the abduction investigators were sure that the perpetrators could be found in a certain area of Hannibal—a neighbourhood deeply affected by drug-related crimes. It was a section of town that, to the displeasure of the criminals, the police department had a constant presence in as they continued their search for Christina.

"With the police there they could not deal drugs, so they started to inform investigators about what had happened just to make the police leave again," Cindy explains. "It quickly turned out that this group of people had taken Christina and forced her into prostitution in Peoria, Illinois. She had become a victim of human trafficking."

PICTURE OF A DAUGHTER

Although the tips about Christina's disappearance had come from criminals who had an interest in shifting the police's focus to another city, Cindy believes that the information was valid. Because soon after the police received those tips, Cindy also started receiving information from law-abiding citizens saying that Christina had been seen in Peoria on numerous occasions.

A waitress reported that three weeks after her disappearance, Christina had come into Raedene's Country Cafe outside of Peoria. In a very shaken manner, she asked for help. But before the waitress could ask what was wrong Christina ran off again.

After that, the tips were suddenly so numerous and seemed so trustworthy that Christina's family hired a private investigator. Like the local police department, the PI tracked several leads to Peoria, which was a much larger city than Hannibal and a two-and-a-half-hour drive from Christina's home.

"I would always be completely crushed when we heard of a lead and it turned out to be wrong," Cindy explains.

Shortly after the first tips came in, Cindy went to Peoria to help search for Christina. Her search brought her to a part of the city where most people would never voluntarily go.

"She is reported to be in an area that is very dangerous, with a lot of drugs and violence. But when your child is missing," Cindy explains, "you will go anywhere. I never pay much attention to my own safety when searching for Christina. The only thing I focus on is getting her back home," she says.

Cindy, along with her husband Alex, moved to Peoria for a period of time to intensify their search efforts. The couple sold most of their belongings so they could finance their search, which unfortunately took them in many directions.

Cindy explains that she would often have dreams about specific houses, addresses, and streets in Peoria. Afterwards, she would follow up on her dreams by visiting the places she had imagined…but her investigations never led to anything.

After Cindy had spent several months living in campgrounds around Peoria, her finances had run their course. Without money she was unable to continue the search, and she had to return to Hannibal without Christina. And with her daughter still missing, Cindy also now had the responsibility of looking after Christina's daughter, Alexandria.

After the abduction Alexandria's life changed dramatically. She no longer had the mother to nurture and comfort her needs. Alexandria's father was already living with two older daughters from a previous marriage, so Cindy offered to take care of her grandchild. Thus for the first five years after Christina's disappearance, Alexandria stayed with Cindy. Somehow, the granddaughter also took care of the grandmother.

"Alexandria helped me through the first years," Cindy acknowledges frankly. "She was the last we had left of Christina. She looks like her, she acts like her and has her spirit. She has brought so much joy to my life during sad times." Today, Alexandria lives with her dad again.

Although Cindy had to help raise Alexandria she never stopped looking for her own daughter. Ten years after the abduction she still frequently travels to Peoria to resume her search. Often, she receives information that places Christina within an area of the city that is thirty blocks long.

Cindy feels absolutely certain that Christina is alive and in Peoria. A store clerk reported she had met Christina in her shop, and a police officer told local media that he believes he has seen her. The officer explained that he had even tried to approach her; however, she had fled before he could get to her. Christina, the officer explained, seemed scared.

Cindy says that the different tips the case has garnered has convinced her that human traffickers are responsible for taking Christina. The mother says she also knows this because she spoke to a woman who explained she met Christina after she had checked herself in to a mental hospital in Peoria. The woman was a patient at the time, and she described Christina as being fragile and suicidal. According to her, Christina told the hospital that she had been raped and molested, which had resulted in a pregnancy. Once Christina's pimp found out about the pregnancy, he beat her up so badly that she miscarried.

The woman also explained that Christina had told her that she had been abducted, that she was forced into prostitution, and that she had been controlled for years by a single pimp. Previously she had been sold numerous times, passed among the traffickers. And Cindy is sure that the woman was talking about her daughter. During their conversation the woman mentioned she had seen an old "missing persons" flyer in Christina's purse. On the flyer was a picture of Alexandria. Cindy explains that she always puts pictures of Alexandria on the fliers to help Christina remember—and miss—her daughter. She hopes this will motivate Christina to return home one day.

After being released from the hospital, the woman told police about her meeting with Christina. Today, local law enforcement is so sure that Christina is in the area that they have intensified their search for Christina. The police are even offering a reward of $1,000 dollars for information that leads to Christina's exact location. By the end of 2018, the police department had also produced a missing persons video about Christina to raise public awareness regarding the case.

As a result of reports stating that Christina has moved freely within Peoria, people have often asked Cindy why her daughter does not leave her captors; but according to her mother victims of human trafficking find it difficult to escape their traffickers, because right from the start the traffickers break down their victims' self-esteem. They bully them through violence, often leaving them scared and vulnerable, and too afraid to return to their homes. At the same time, the traffickers get their victims addicted to drugs such as heroin. Once drugs are involved it becomes even more difficult for human trafficking victims to get away. Therefore Cindy believes that Christina is scared, and that she may have accepted a life that involves being controlled by either a human trafficking ring or pimps.

Cindy says only one thing can make Christina come back home. A personal encounter between mother and daughter.

"I have to look her in the eyes and assure [her] that we can protect her. I hope God prepares her mind for that moment," Cindy explains.

ANYONE CAN BECOME A VICTIM

Prior to Christina's abduction Cindy barely knew anything about human trafficking, which has become a risk factor for many people across the United States…and the rest of the world. Over the years Cindy has developed her knowledge of human trafficking, which Homeland Security describes as:

> *A modern-day slavery that involves the use of force, fraud, or coercion to obtain some type of labor or commercial sex act.*

> *Every year, millions of men, women, and children are trafficked in countries around the world, including the United States. Human trafficking is a hidden crime as victims rarely come forward to seek help because of language barriers, fear of the traffickers, and/or fear of law enforcement.*

> *Traffickers look for people who are susceptible for a variety of reasons, including psychological or emotional vulnerability,*

economic hardship, lack of a social safety net, natural disas-
ters, or political instability. The trauma caused by the traffick-
ers can be so great that many may not identify themselves as
victims or ask for help, even in highly public settings.

(Source: *www.dhs.gov*)

According to Cindy, her daughter's story supports Homeland Security's description in many ways. Christina was probably chosen by the abductors because of her fragile psyche. The traumas she has suffered from being beaten, raped, and forced to take drugs is believed to have prevented her from asking for help to escape her traffickers.

Since 2007, more than 45,000 victims' cases have been reported to the National Human Trafficking Hotline in the United States. Notably, the victims come from all states, and from the streets of New York to the streets of Peoria. The U.S. government estimates that human trafficking is a $32 billion-a-year industry for criminal organisations in the United States, and that as many as 300,000 Americans under the age of eighteen are lured into the commercial sex trade every year. Approximately 80 percent of all people being bought, sold, and imprisoned in the underground sex service industry are women and children. The life expectancy of a victim of human trafficking is seven years, after which time the victim is often found dead from physical assault, a drug overdose, or suicide. A victim's average age is eleven to fourteen years, according to government sources.

"Anyone from anywhere can be a victim of human trafficking, even in a small peaceful place like Hannibal with seventeen thousand inhabitants," Cindy explains. "We need to realise this and be on guard with our children. Unfortunately, most people are not aware of how big a problem human trafficking and sex exploitation has become in America. Today, it is a big industry [for] criminals, and therefore it is also difficult to battle because they protect their business," Cindy notes, trying to explain why it is so difficult for victims to escape once they are trapped.

In Cindy's opinion law enforcement needs to allocate more resources to combat the problem of human trafficking, and, in general, the public needs to become more aware of the problem to help prevent it. However, believing that this kind of modern slavery exists is difficult unless you are a victim of it, Cindy acknowledges.

"When Christina was a child I was overprotective with her, but never in my wildest dream had I imagined that she would one day be kidnapped and sold as a sex slave," she says.

After losing Christina, Cindy became involved with other parents who are also searching for their loved ones. Today, Cindy says the number of people who are missing in America is unreal. But she also says that many of the missing people have a chance to come home.

"A majority of [time], someone knows what has happened, but they don't come forward with their knowledge, and by keeping silent they are also hurting families, parents, and—not least [in importance]— the children. Try to imagine what it is like for a kid to be trapped and abused by a stranger. People who know about abductions must come forward. No one is entitled to take someone's child. It is unbelievable how much evil [is] targeted towards our children. Even family members sell their relatives for money and hurt those who love them. And if you keep silent you are an accomplice," Cindy asserts.

Despite missing her daughter she feels fortunate in comparison to many other parents of missing persons, because she at least has evidence of her daughter's whereabouts. Most families do not.

"Many will never know if their child is trapped or dead. We were lucky to get leads and proof of Christina being alive so quick after her disappearance. That has given me a lot of comfort," Cindy says.

OBSESSED WITH SEARCHING

Cindy has lost many important people in her life—among others, her parents. Still missing, Christina hurts in a way Cindy never thought was possible.

"I really did not know pain till I lost Christina. When she was abducted I was just screaming and feeling awful all the time. I still do," she says.

After a while Cindy developed post-traumatic stress disorder (PTSD) from the tormenting experiences she has gone through. As a consequence she has lost her ability to remember most parts of her life.

"I could not even remember what hospital we went to when Christina was born. I had to go back and look at the birth certificate," she says.

One of the things that has caused her to develop a feeling of constant, traumatic stress has been visualising what might have happened to Christina while she remained in the possession of the kidnappers.

"I became insane when thinking of what they were doing to her. If she was beaten, drugged or raped. I can't let myself go there anymore. I simply lose it," Cindy says. She recalls that a couple of years ago, on Christina's birthday (March 28), she had a complete breakdown. After that incident she had to step down because her mental state could not take any more. Until then, she had always been out there, looking for her daughter, no matter whether it was her birthday, Thanksgiving, or Christmas.

"My health is very bad and [is] affected by her missing. It is all about her and never myself. The first six years I was obsessed with searching for her. And today I know I have done everything humanly possible to find her," Cindy says, adding that the family has also suffered. They have sustained financial hardships and lost their vehicles, their camper, and their belongings, because they have spent all their money on their private investigation, trying to find Christina.

"We just got rid of all material things so we could afford looking for her. But money does not matter. The worst has been the mental cost," the mother says.

Cindy is not the only member of the family who struggles to get through life. Christina was very close to her brother Brian, who is four years older than Christina. According to Cindy, Brian has suffered from depression and, since his sister's disappearance, never leaves home.

"He really struggles," Cindy says.

However, the person suffering the most is probably Alexandria, who was just six months old when she lost her mother. Although she never really knew Christina, the thought of her mom being held captive brings a lot of pain into her life. Especially when she sees how close other ten-year-olds are to their mothers. Cindy explains:

"It is getting harder for her all the time. She breaks down and doesn't understand why she does not have a mama when all the other children have one. Often, she cries herself to sleep just screaming 'Mom, Mom, Mom.'"

Although Alexandria suffers terribly from not knowing what happened to her mother, the young girl has still found the strength to share her sorrow. A few years ago relatives of the approximately nine hundred people who are missing in Missouri gathered to remember their loved ones. At that event Alexandria took the stage to share a few words about her mother.

"I feel sad because my mommy is missing," Alexandria said, according to the local newspaper, *Fulton Sun*. "I miss her being here for everything. I ask Jesus to please bring her back because I miss her so much in my heart. I just really want all this to be over with so I can have my mommy back."

Cindy says that in spite of her suffering, Alexandria has a very generous character…just like her mother.

Christina was the type of person who could not pass a homeless person without giving him her last dollar, and she was always very attentive to others' needs. She once gave up her job as a waitress to help her grandmother when she became sick. However, Christina was not present when her grandmother died. By that time she had already been taken.

"She loved her grandmother so much, and in general she just had a big heart. She got along with everybody, and it is unthinkable someone could have been angry with her when she disappeared," Cindy says reassuringly.

She also says that her daughter always kept her word and her promises to others.

"We could always trust in her, and she always came home as planned," Cindy says. "Especially to her baby that she loved so much," she adds.

Leading up to the abduction, nothing in Christina's behaviour indicated anything was wrong, or that she did not feel the same way she always felt, Cindy says.

A WARNING

Although the mother has not given up on searching for her daughter she today accepts that the chances of finding Christina are limited. Therefore she has turned to God for strength.

"I hurt every day. Night after night I lay down not knowing where my child is. As human beings we can only bear a certain amount of pain, and when I broke down I had to give it all to God. Today my faith carries me through. I have to believe God has all this planned out, and that one day investigators will call to tell they finally got her," Cindy says, keeping her faith alive.

Until that day Cindy tries to stay close to her daughter in spirit, although she says it's getting harder and harder. She says she always had a certain connection with her daughter. If Cindy were feeling sad, Christina would automatically call to check up on her mom. They simply had a spiritual feeling for each other.

"But it feels like this connection has faded over the last few years," Cindy notes. "Today I feel she is spiritually dead, but yet still alive. When I am in Peoria the feel of being connected and close to her returns. So leaving the city is the loneliest feeling. Every time I go home I cry because I feel I am letting Christina down."

Therefore, as soon as she gets back home, she always writes letters to Christina explaining her thoughts, feelings, and actions. The letters are printed on the missing persons flyers, along with both old and recent photos of Alexandria. Cindy hopes that Christina reads the fliers once in a while, so she knows that her family has not given up on her.

"We never will," Cindy vows, "and I hope she just feels like calling one day, or that she perhaps has the chance to set up a Facebook page to write me. I am very careful about how I approach her because I am sure she is being watched all the time and therefore it is difficult for her to leave physically, but perhaps she has the chance of getting online," Cindy states hopefully.

Until that day Cindy will continue to think about whether she should approach the people who are believed to have kidnapped her daughter, and ask if she can have her back.

"People have warned me about the perpetrators, because they are very dangerous, but what more can they do to me? They have already taken everything from me. In the beginning I even thought about shooting one of them, but today I do not want to harm them, and I would not know how to," Cindy says.

Immediately after the abduction Cindy was also very determined to make sure the perpetrators were punished for their crimes, but today that is not important to her.

"If someone goes to jail it is just icing on the cake. I just want Christina back," the mother says, "and I know that one day she will be coming home. We get so many leads and one of them will lead me to her."

4

FAMILY ABDUCTIONS

Every year more than 200,000 American children become victims of a family abduction: they are kidnapped or concealed by a parent or another family member who violated another person's custodial or visitation rights.

The National Center for Missing and Exploited Children has reviewed cases of 16,264 children who were abducted by a parent or family member between 2008 and 2018. Almost two-thirds of the victims were between the ages of 0 and 6 years…and their mothers were most likely to be the abductor. In fact, mothers accounted for 54 percent of all family abductions while fathers accounted for 36 percent. In the remaining cases the abductor was another family member (not a parent) related to the victim. Still, women are most often the abductor and account for 60 percent of all family-related abduction cases.

Most often, the children who are victims of a family abduction are returned safely to their home. Only 5 percent of the cases the National Center for Missing and Exploited Children reviewed have not been solved. In those cases, the abducted child is still missing.

However, the claim that family abductions aren't harmful to the child—because, after all, they are with a family member—is a myth. Often, a child is not abducted as a result of the perpetrator's love for the child, but out of anger or the desire for vengeance against a spouse. The parent or family member who abducts the child also often has a history of marital instability, domestic violence, or child abuse. And when the perpetrator abducts the child, the abductor's problems increase, inflicting further harm and damage to the child.

After the abduction, the parent often has no job, struggles financially, moves residences a lot, and keeps the child in hiding—outside of any interaction with the surrounding community—harming the child's social skills and the possibility that the child will have a healthy upbringing, as the children who are victims of family abductions are at times prevented from obtaining medical care. Parents have even been known to dress the child in clothes that do not conform to the child's gender, and to raise the child as though the child is a member of the opposite sex, in order to try to hide the child's true identity.

A majority of all children abducted by parents or family members are quickly returned to the parent who has custody rights of the child. In the cases reviewed by the National Center for Missing and Exploited Children, the mean duration of time the abducted children were missing for was six months. But not all children who are victims of family abductions are returned that quickly.

For more than three decades, Louis Zaharias has been searching for his two children, **Christopher** and **Lisa Mae**, who were abducted by their mother. Since the perpetrator of family abductions is most likely to be the abducted child's mother, the example given here is told through the father's eyes.

A HOME OF SADNESS

Missing: Christopher Louis Zaharias and Lisa Mae Zaharias
Dates of Birth: Christopher, 03/25/1984; Lisa Mae, 08/18/1986
Missing From: Mission Viejo, California
Missing Since: 11/20/1987 (3 years old and 1 year old)
Classification: Family Abduction
Interview: Louis Zaharias, father of Christopher and Lisa Mae

When Louis walked into Western State University he was determined to focus on his studies. However, his mind quickly wandered off as he laid eyes on the girl at the reception desk. Love had struck on the first day of law school in Fullerton, California, on August 22, 1977.

Susan was without doubt the most beautiful girl Louis had ever seen, and instead of making his way to the law library he approached the receptionist.

"She was my thunderbolt, as we Italians call it," Louis says. "I just could not help it. I walked straight up to her, introduced myself, and invited her out. But my Bronx accent was so heavy that she thought I introduced myself as Huey and not Louie. Afterwards she would always tease me in a loving way by calling me Huey." The Italian man laughs as if it were only yesterday when he fell in love with Susan.

But when he is brought back to the present day, forty-two years after first falling for Susan, his voice trembles, and he breaks down in tears. Because love would soon turn to estrangement and a lifetime of grief that not even Louis' tough upbringing could have prepared him for.

Louis grew up in the Bronx, and when he was seventeen years old his father abandoned the family. Louis was so saddened by his father's actions that he began to cultivate a violent and angry nature.

"In the streets of New York I saw everything from race riots to random violence. And I participated myself. I became a very aggressive and combative kid. All my knuckles were broken, I had my teeth knocked out, my nose broken, and I was stabbed twice. It was a very tough life," Louis recalls of his childhood in the Bronx, where violence and drug abuse were each other's daily companions.

Like most of his friends who grew up in the 1960s and 1970s, Louis became a drug user at an early age. When the twenty-three-year-old New Yorker matriculated at Western State University nothing indicated he would live to become an old man.

"But when I met Susan," Louis recalls, "she brought humanity and warmth into my life, and she changed my perspective."

At the beginning of their relationship both Louis and Susan did drugs, one time to the extent that Louis overdosed. Susan saved his life.

"Susan gave me CPR and a solution of valium. Susan is the reason I am alive today. For that I will always be grateful," Louis says.

However, Susan's parents were not grateful. They did not approve of their daughter's new boyfriend, because he was an Italian-Catholic from the Bronx. Louis' background did not fit in with their values and their way of life in Oklahoma, Louis recalls.

"They were white Anglo-Saxon Baptists leading the life of rich oil people. And they did not like an Italian greaseball like me," he says.

Susan's family therefore gave their daughter an ultimatum. Either she would leave Louis, or they would leave her.

"She chose me, and it aroused their anger," Louis recalls. "They accused me of having stolen their daughter, and they wanted revenge at any cost."

Louis says Susan was hurt by her family's ultimatum, and that several times she tried to restore the relationship, writing letters to her parents, telling them of her love for Louis and begging them to accept him.

"She would write the letters with me sitting next to her. She really tried to make things right," Louis says.

A letter from Susan's private collection written in April 1979 said:

Dear mom, I hope you don't take anything I say wrong, but I just have to speak my mind. It has been building up for a year now and I won't let it go for another year without making at least one last plea. It has been one year since I have seen you and I really can't believe you have carried your hatred for that long. When will you stop this? When will you accept Louis? He never made me leave home. I wanted to so I could be with him all the time…

Susan insisted on restoring the relationship with her family. And her family slowly started communicating with her after they received Susan's letters. Louis also wrote letters to help with the reconciliation, but they were ignored, he says.

"They hated me. For the ten years I was together with Susan I had no name. They would always refer to me as 'the Italian greaseball', and I was never invited for any family events. When we got engaged and married they also refused to come to either celebration," Louis says.

He says that from the very beginning Susan's family embarked on a mission to destroy the family he and Susan were creating. Louis asserts that Susan's family even tried to kidnap Susan a year after the couple met.

"We were visiting her aunt, and before I could get in the house they slammed the door shut and locked Susan up against her will. I could not get inside the house, and I had to call local Villa Park police, who forced them to open up," Louis says.

LOCKED IN THE CAR

Despite their troubled family life Louis and Susan were determined to create their own family. In 1984 Susan gave birth to their first child.

"When I held Christopher in my arms for the first time, I felt like I was holding God," Louis tenderly recalls.

He felt blessed that Susan had given him the child—a baby that, living the life of a drug addict, he never dared to dream of. But after the birth of Christopher, having a family and Susan's love made him give up his everyday drug use. Louis went into rehab, and in 1982 he got a job in New York. Everything was for the first time moving in the right direction. Suddenly he could be the father he never felt he had himself.

Two years after Christopher was born, Lisa Mae joined the family.

"My own mom had a tough life, but when she had grandchildren I saw the change," Louis says. "She became a happy person, and she adored Susan for having brought her grandkids. She adored her more than she had ever adored anyone else," he says.

For Susan, life as a mother of two small children was hard, in spite of being loved and adored.

First, the couple tried making things right in 1985 by moving to Mission Viejo, California, where Louis was offered a new position. Susan felt pleased about the move, as the California girl never could stand the cold and snow in New York. But the move could not shift the pain she felt as a result of her parents' disapproval of Louis and the stress motherhood brought into her life.

"She was overwhelmed with two kids. And I was not there to help her," Louis acknowledges. "Two years after moving back I started a new job, and I was away fourteen to fifteen hours every day. At the same time, Susan suffered postpartum depression traumas from her pregnancy, and she began self-medicating. That triggered her addiction."

According to Louis his wife became a far worse drug addict than he had been; it did not help that they would occasionally use together. Whenever an anniversary or a holiday came around, Louis' mother would take care of the children while the parents escaped to a nearby hotel.

"I had gotten out of smoking what today is known as crack. I overcame the day-to-day addiction by the help of Susan. But at times we would have our 'vice' weekend. We would get an eight ball of cocaine, go to a hotel, and have a sex-party weekend. Besides that we always smoked pot, but after becoming a father I never did mushrooms, acid, or any other hard drugs again," Louis says.

Instead, his wife started doing hard-core drugs like cocaine and crystal meth, according to Louis. He says he eventually discovered that while he was working, a typical day for his wife would entail putting the kids in the car and driving with them from drug dealer to drug dealer.

"The kids were locked in the car from morning to evening while she was doing drugs. Later, her two closest friends would even give sworn testimonies about this," Louis says.

It was not until people came knocking on his door that he realised how addicted his wife had become. When they knocked, they wanted money. Susan was in charge of paying the family's bills, but she paid the local drug dealers with Louis' paycheque instead. His wife's addiction became even more obvious the day the water company came to collect an outstanding debt. It turned out Susan had committed cheque fraud in the amount of more than $6,000. Louis says the sheriff's Fraud Unit came to his house sometime in November 1987 to arrest Susan. That was a few days before she took off with the children.

"My mother had come out to look after the children," Louis recalls, "and when she opened the door there was no longer any chance of Susan hiding [the fact] that she had been spending our money on drugs instead of paying the bills. Suddenly, we owed everyone money, and she committed credit card fraud trying to cover it up," Louis says.

When he came home that night he confronted Susan. An argument broke out between the couple. Louis spent the night on the couch, but when he woke up in the morning he never imagined how the day would end.

Louis says that that morning, Susan started kicking and hitting him. A neighbour later testified to having seen the attack, dispelling the allegations of domestic violence Susan filed against Louis.

"She was ninety-five pounds, I was over two hundred pounds but I could not stop her. Thank God a neighbour saw her attacking me, so I was not the only one who knew what was happening. I just [told myself] 'I have to get out of here' because I did not want to hit her back. I just wanted to calm things down and go to work. But I could not go there because my arms and neck were bleeding," Louis says.

Instead, he checked in to a motel and cleaned up and hoped that his mother would be able to calm Susan down by the time he went back home a few hours later.

When he came home Louis realised that he was not the only one who had been assaulted. According to Louis his mother was lying on the sidewalk when he approached the house.

"Susan had beat the shit out of her and just left her by herself in the street," Louis says. He suspects that Susan combined cocaine and methamphetamine earlier that morning; the combination of drugs would have made her extremely aggressive. But it also apparently made her take off with the kids.

"On November twentieth, 1987, my nightmare began when I suddenly became the victim of parental family abduction. I might have had a tough upbringing, but never as a child did I suffer the pain I now would as an adult," Louis says about the day on which he sought help from authorities.

A TERRIBLE MISPERCEPTION

Each year more than 200,000 children are abducted by family members. Most of them come home shortly after being taken. But back in the 1980s, before the days of AMBER alerts, law enforcement hesitated launching big investigations immediately after a disappearance when dealing with family abduction cases. Often, it was difficult to determine, right away, which parent was entitled to be with the kids and what the reasons were when a parent took off with a child.

"Law enforcement felt it was a civil, domestic matter," Louis says.

Furthermore, Louis says that in the late 1980s there was a dark shadow hanging over any issue relating to the relationship between a husband and his wife. The husband was automatically considered the guilty one when things went wrong, Louis says. He adds that only in recent years has it been generally acknowledged that women can also be violent and unfit as parents.

"Back then it was horrible. It took a long time before police realised that my kids had been abducted, that it was serious, and that I was the victim. In the beginning they considered me a wife beater, and that was why she had taken off. However, I am forever grateful to the witness who came forward to reveal the truth of the situation," Louis says.

He filed a parental kidnapping police report, but Susan had gone to a relative's house in Riverside, California, where she filed a fraudulent domestic violence report against Louis, saying she was hiding the children from him on that basis.

It took more than forty days to convince the police that Louis was not guilty. Only then, in mid-February of 1988, did law enforcement finally issue a warrant for Susan's arrest.

"While waiting for the police to wake up we lost important time in the search for my kids. Forty days is a lifetime when it comes to searching for abducted children, and when the police got things straight Susan had taken off. Had police acted right in the beginning they could have gone directly to Riverside and picked up the kids. End of story. Now the nightmare has continued for more than thirty-one years," Louis says.

According to Louis, law enforcement later admitted to their mistakes. In 2007, he received an email from the assistant district attorney handling the case, saying that if law enforcement had known in the beginning what they know now they would have dealt with the case in a completely different way.

"But it does not help me that they admit twenty years later they screwed up. I needed their help back then," Louis says.

According to Louis, when the crimes occurred it also was difficult for him to earn the sympathy and help of other people. When people hear a child has been taken by another parent, they often ask: "How bad can it be?" Louis says.

According to him this question arises out of a terrible misperception.

"They think the other parent had good reasons for taking the children, and, after all, they are still with a parent. But it is quite bad. Often, the children are taken by a parent that is abusing drugs, that is abusing the child, and [that isn't] the children's primary parent in the first place. It is unbelievable that a parent can inflict such an abuse on their own children. They take the children out of selfishness. Not love," Louis says.

From his own experience as a drug abuser, Louis knew the danger being on the run with Susan posed to Christopher and Lisa Mae. According to Louis, Susan suffered from a heart condition and needed treatment. Louis was afraid she would not get it while living in hiding. So to survive she would need the help of other people, and Louis never doubted where she would get it.

"When she started abusing drugs she became vulnerable and paranoid. She was an easy target when her family began to influence her mind. I am not in doubt they set her up [for] taking the kids away," Louis candidly states.

He knew that Susan's use of cocaine and methamphetamine had made her paranoid, and he says Susan's family preyed on her fear when they told her that he was going to take the children away from her as a result of the drug abuse and stolen money.

"They believed I stole their daughter ten years earlier—and now they would steal her back. It was the perfect revenge for them," Louis says.

Therefore Louis is sure that Susan's parents, together with other family members, planned the abduction. He is certain, too, that when she left the house in Riverside her parents helped her onto a plane, thereby escaping the authorities in California. And today Louis accuses law enforcement of never having investigated her family's part in the kidnapping. Therefore Louis had filed civil lawsuits against the family for custodial interference. Due to jurisdictional issues, Louis has had to file lawsuits in California, Pennsylvania, and Oklahoma. And he had to hire lawyers in each state. The fight was uneven.

"Susan comes from a very wealthy family with a lot of oil money, so we were up against different teams of lawyers. They covered us in paperwork and I could not pay the bills," Louis says.

LOVE OUTWEIGHS ANGER

During the lawsuits, family members testified that they had helped Susan leave California and that they later provided her with money while she was on the run with the children. Louis asked the district attorney of Orange County, California, why he did not press charges against the family for aiding Susan in the kidnapping, and he says that in 1988 he received a letter in response to his question. The letter claimed that it was not the policy of law enforcement to prosecute family members who render "minor" assistance to a kidnapper.

"I still have that letter among the more than two thousand pounds of documents that I keep in my apartment about the case," Louis says.

Louis further claims that Susan's family kept orchestrating fraudulent stories about him. One story said he was part of the Italian Mafia, and that he had put a contract on Susan's head. Therefore she was now hiding with the children.

"And they said that I had handcuffed her and kept her locked up in the garage," Louis says.

He thinks it's suspicious that Susan's family has never hired private investigators to search for their grandchildren. He claims they never had the desire to because they have all along known where the children are, and that they have probably seen them occasionally.

"I am sure they know where they have been all this time," Louis says, even though he admits that he still bears a grudge against Susan's family, and that at times he has speculated about what he would like to do to them.

"But how would it serve my children if I went and killed her relatives? Then my kids would have two criminal parents. Once I had the guns and the anger to do so, but my love for my children outweighs the anger no matter what they did to my children. But it takes energy and sheer will to suppress the anger I have inside me. Still, the love for my children is always the blanket on the flame. But her family should thank God that I never stop loving my kids and fall into despair," Louis confesses.

Despite the harm Susan has caused, Louis refuses to say he hates her. Instead he feels sorry for her—and also blames himself for what happened.

"I am very sad that I could not help Susan the way she helped me when I was the coke addict. She saved me, and I would have liked to have saved her. Despite the fact I could always spot a drug user no matter where I was in the world, I could not when there was a drug user living in my house. I blame myself for not having helped her, because I truly loved her," Louis says.

Therefore, in the beginning, he also had difficulties acknowledging that the love of his life had abducted his children.

"For six months after [they had been taken] I still wore my wedding ring. One day my boss said: 'Take it off or I will fire you.' He was more angry at her than I was," Louis says.

In the wake of his split from Susan, Louis has met other women, but the relationships always come to a premature end. The women always tell him that they can feel he is still in love with Susan.

"And I always reply to them by asking: How do you stop loving a person that has saved your life and that gave you babies? I still love that person, but I also hate the Frankenstein she turned into when she took my babies," Louis says.

When asked how he would react if he were ever to see Susan again, his reaction comes promptly.

"I would probably just break down and cry and ask her why? Why did she not come asking me for help back then?" Louis says.

He will, however, forever have to live with the devastation Susan's actions have had on his body, mind, and soul. When Susan kidnapped the kids, Louis was a young man who could bench 400 pounds. Today he is an old man who can barely carry himself. Because when you live with grief for decades you develop other diseases. Today, Louis suffers from post-traumatic stress disorder (PTSD). He has also been diagnosed with bipolar disorder, and he suffers from a heart condition. These are a few of the many physical ailments that have developed from the stress of the kidnapping. As Louis says:

"Mental and emotional pain breaks the body and mind down in every possible way."

And his pain begins as soon as he opens his eyes every day. The first thing he does in the morning is vomit—a physical reaction to the question of how he is going to get through another day. These daily episodes are intense and exhausting.

"My life is like a blender full of all sorts of emotions. The only [sure] thing is that my emotions are stirring around all the time. It is just too much to handle, and I have broken down several times. I could not take it anymore around Christmastime in 2013. I was in a very bad state of mind, and I was hospitalised. For an entire year I was on mental disability," Louis acknowledges.

This was not the first time Louis broke down. He has often contemplated suicide because, according to Louis, the pain can reach a level where he just wants to be without the hurt.

"I have had the gun in my mouth," he says.

Another night he took the gun and put three rounds in the chamber, which could hold six bullets. It was fifty-fifty whether Louis was going to survive.

"When I pulled the trigger it fell on an empty chamber. God wanted me to live. He wanted me here, searching for my children, and since that day I have maintained hope that I am going to find them, even though I still at times feel like killing myself. But you can say that the love for my children is stronger than my desire to relieve myself of the pain I feel," Louis says.

LIFE IN THE GHETTO

Today, Louis still fights to get his children back, and he says his case is no longer an abduction case, but a murder case.

"When they stole my children, they killed everything inside of me. I am a walking dead man," Louis explains.

He says he has tried everything possible to get his children back; often, the efforts have brought new hope. In the summer of 2017, the National Center for Missing and Exploited Children and the advertising company Clear Channel put up 1,000 electronic billboards across America. For four weeks the billboards lit up the sky…and Louis' hopes that they would help identify where his children were. But as had often happened before, his hopes were extinguished.

"I never have closure. I have been trapped in this state of mind for thirty years without knowing what happened to my children. Today, I don't know if they are safe, if they are parents, or even if they are dead. Not knowing is an indescribable pain that I live with daily," Louis says.

His search has also brought impoverishment. Louis has spent over a million dollars on private investigators, lawyers, and other means of trying to get his children back. A few years back his financial condition forced Louis to live in the slums, where he had a small apartment with only a mattress on the floor, as he could not afford any other furniture.

"The cockroaches were crawling all over me, and I woke up in the middle of the night with rats biting my toes. The place was so infested that I could not have food in the apartment, because if I did it would right away be flooded with cockroaches and rats," Louis says.

Living in the ghetto posed a health risk in other ways. Five times, police had to come and save Louis as he was assaulted by other neighbours struggling to get through life by robbing other people. Louis describes the ordeal he went through as six months in hell. With the help of friends he eventually made it out of the ghetto. But he still lives in poverty.

"I still spend all my money on finding my kids. Therefore I have one mug and one plate. I have nothing, but no one knows because no one comes to my home because it is a home of sadness and a home of isolation. The only time I see people is when I go to work," Louis says.

After leaving the ghetto he continued his job as a senior law clerk. Despite going to law school he never got his bar licence as a lawyer because he could not afford it after Susan left with the children.

"I often walk around with wet socks from rain, because my shoes are full of holes, but I cannot afford new shoes. When I go to work my pants are also full of holes—at a prestigious law firm! But my bosses know what happened, and they are kind enough to hold on to me," Louis says.

And by Louis' own admission the firm can expect him to be there for a long time, if they will let him. Louis says he is sixty-five years old, and that he will never be able to retire, due to his financial situation.

"Last time I checked I had thirty-three cents in my saving accounts. So I will die at my desk or put a bullet to my head if I do not find my children and can no longer care for myself," Louis admits.

Despite the warnings of his premature death, Louis is trying to maintain hope. He just wants to see his children one more time before he dies.

"I gotta see them, hear their voices, and just hold them. I want to see who they have become, and to make sure they are all right. Not knowing if I will see them before I die is living in terror. The same is not knowing if they have died," Louis says.

He believes that immediately after the kidnapping Susan took the children to a gravesite and told them their father was dead so they would not search for him as they got older, or she would have painted their father to be the worst monster of all time so they would not have any desire to look him up. Parental alienation syndrome is often a parental kidnapper's most effective weapon.

"But none of [that] is true. I am a loving father that miss[es] my kids every day, and I will do anything for them," Louis avows.

Louis also says that today he is not only fighting for his own kids but all American children who are in danger of being abducted. He does that by raising positive awareness of his case. And he has made landmark Supreme Court case law and written legislation for the state of Oklahoma.

"People have told me they contemplated kidnapping their children, but after hearing my story they have realised that is not the way [to go] about things. No parents should lose a child," Louis says, adding that he believes he has been given a mission that he can fulfill only if he shows the world who Louis Zaharias is, for good and for ill.

"I cannot buy people's loyalty, and if I am caught in just one lie I lose everything. Therefore I have told all about my flaws and the bad person I was. My honesty is all I have, though letting out all the skeletons [in] the closets has done a lot of damage to me and my career," Louis says.

HAPPY AND PROUD

After the abduction Louis moved to Arizona, where he worked as a kindergarten teacher for seven years. Later he also worked as a paralegal for the Maricopa County District Attorney's office. Given Louis' background as a child advocate and a kindergarten teacher, the DA's office assigned him to the Child Abuse Unit for two years before he decided to move back to California. Working with the district attorney was shocking for Louis in many ways.

"District attorney's offices are pretty much the same everywhere. And I found out that district attorneys do not prosecute crimes because someone broke the law. They only prosecute crimes based on politics, trends, and when they know they will get a good conviction rate. I have lost a lot of faith in our justice system, and I also want to tell people about the flaws within it," Louis says.

Though he feels that life has been unfair to him he tries to find strength by telling himself there is a reason for his suffering.

"Sometimes God asks us to do hard things," Louis says, "and perhaps he asked me to do good for millions of people. God has given me broad shoulders."

By telling his story Louis hopes people realise not only the harsh toll parental abductions have on the other parent but, more importantly, how they harm their own children. According to Louis, the trauma inflicted on many abducted children will follow them forever.

"Some [parental kidnappers] dress up boys as girls to hide their identity," Louis says, "and some of the children even become afraid of daylight, because they are only allowed out at night when no one will see them. Too many children have also been killed in high-speed chases when parents have stolen and taken off with them. So many children are suffering by their parent's evil, and if I can save just one child by telling my story, I will be happy and proud."

In the 1980s, after the U.S. Congress held hearings on the subject of parental kidnapping, they declared parental kidnappings to be one of the most heinous forms of child abuse any person can engage in.

5

INFANT ABDUCTIONS

The young black female identified herself as Latoya when she kindly offered to change April Williams' diaper so her exhausted mother could rest. Minutes later "Latoya" ran off with the three-month-old baby. April's abduction received wide attention because the abduction occurred at a Washington, DC, bus station only a few blocks from the White House, while April and her mother were in transit. More than three decades later, the case still remains unsolved.

April's kidnapping received a lot of attention not only because it happened so close to the U.S. president's residence, but also because infant abduction cases are very rare.

The National Center for Missing and Exploited Children registered only 325 cases of abducted infants in the United States that took place between 1965 and 2018.

An infant abduction is defined as a kidnapping of a child under six months of age. This type of abduction can take various forms, from a noncustodial parent abducting the infant to a stranger abducting a child from a hospital, a home, or a public place. A review of the 325 cases mentioned previously shows that:

- *140 infants were taken from health care facilities*

- *138 infants were taken from their home*

- *47 infants were abducted in locations other than health care facilities or their homes*

- *16 infants still remain missing*

Based on the information gleaned from these cases, the National Center for Missing and Exploited Children has tried to create a composite portrait of infant abductors. Usually, the centre says, the abductor is a female of childbearing age who appears to be pregnant. Often, she has lost a baby herself or is incapable of becoming pregnant, but she still desires to provide her companion with "his" baby. She usually lives in the community where the abduction takes place, and she visits local nursery and maternity units prior to the abduction. During her visits she asks detailed questions about the babies, procedures, and the maternity floor layout, so she can quickly escape once she has taken the baby. Other times, she pretends to be a health care staff member; often, she becomes friends with the true parents before abducting their child from the health care facility.

The profile of infant abductors who kidnap the child from their home is slightly different than the profile of other abductors. In these cases the abductor is more likely to be single, and she targets a mother she has met at a health care unit. When she carries out the abduction it has already been carefully planned, and she often brings a weapon or impersonates a health care staff member checking on the baby.

Donna Green met an infant abductor just hours after giving birth to her son **Raymond**. A few days later, the abductor showed up unannounced in her home.

AN EMPTY FRAME
Missing: Raymond Lamar Green
Date of Birth: 11/01/1978
Missing From: Atlanta, Georgia
Missing Since: 11/06/1978 (5 days old)
Classification: Endangered Missing
Interview: Donna Green, mother of Raymond

Donna holds a picture frame, but the votive portrait within the frame is not an actual photograph of her son. Instead it is an age-progression drawing, portraying what Raymond might look like today; the only picture Donna has of Raymond is in her mind.

"My son was only five days old when he was abducted. I never had the chance of taking his photo," Donna says. "But I don't need a photo to remember Raymond's beautiful smile as he [lay] in my arms after he was born."

Neither does she need a picture to remember the woman who took him. Donna met her son's abductor a few hours after Raymond's birth. When the proud mother went to watch her seven pound, eight ounce son through the nursery windows of Atlanta's Grady Memorial Hospital, a woman was already there looking at the babies. The woman introduced herself as "Lisa" and pointed at a baby then said it was her niece. Lisa's sister was tired after labour, Lisa told Donna, so Lisa had offered to nurse the baby while her sister regained her strength.

The two women quickly started talking, and Lisa asked which of the babies was Donna's. The proud mother gladly answered. Because why not? Lisa was a young lady in her early twenties with smooth, light skin, warm eyes and a nice smile. The kind of person you would immediately trust, Donna says.

After admiring the babies for half an hour, Lisa suggested she accompany Donna to her room, so they could continue to talk.

Once in the room Lisa asked all sorts of questions about Raymond, and about Donna's background. Donna didn't think much of it. The conversation was pleasant, and Donna was just happy to have made a friend who had an interest in her newborn son.

"I gave her all the information she asked for," Donna admits.

During her second night in hospital Donna was awoken by a strange noise. In the dark she saw Lisa's silhouette. It looked as if she were trying to hide herself in the closet, but when Donna started to move in her hospital bed she quickly disappeared.

"I thought it was strange, but I did not think more of it," she recalls. "I was probably a bit naive."

The next day, Donna's mother came by with a friend to bring her daughter and grandson home. While they were packing Donna's bags, Lisa showed up. She told them that the people who were supposed to take her home had already left, and she would appreciate it if Donna's friend could also give her a ride, since she was going in the same direction. The friend was happy to help, and once he had dropped Donna off at her mother's apartment, he dropped off Lisa.

"This is how she found out where I lived," Donna says.

The following days passed quickly. Donna was only sixteen years old, and she was busy being a mom as Raymond was not her first child. A year earlier she had given birth to her daughter, Raymonda. The young mother was, therefore, exhausted when she heard a knock on the door. To her surprise, Lisa was standing outside. When she opened the door Lisa explained that she had decided to come by to check up on Donna and Raymond.

"I felt it was strange she showed up unannounced," Donna recalls. "Something was not right, but I did not know how to act on that feeling. I was too young to know, and at the same time I also appreciated her concern, so I invited her in."

For an hour they talked, before Donna decided to take a shower. When she left the living room she told her brother, Tony, to look after Raymond.

Tony was the man of the house, even though he was only eighteen years old. And because he was already looking after another sister's newborn son, Mike, Donna imagined he could also look after Raymond.

Shortly after Donna left the room, Raymond started crying. Quickly, Lisa intervened, offering her help. By the time Donna returned from the shower a few minutes later, her brother had dozed off. He was asleep in a chair, together with Mike. There was no sign of Lisa or Raymond.

Confused, Donna rushed to wake up Tony. Once he was awake, Tony told Donna that Lisa had offered to take Raymond outside to keep him from crying.

"It sank in immediately that she had taken Raymond. I just started screaming," Donna says.

She ran quickly out of the apartment to search for Raymond. She met a neighbour in the street who told her she saw a woman with a baby jump into the passenger seat of a brown car before the driver sped off. A crime had been committed—there was no doubt about that—and Lisa was not the only abductor.

"I never blamed my brother," Donna says. "Only myself, because I opened the door and let her in to our home. I led her directly to my baby, and I did not protect him. I failed Raymond," she says.

The subsequent police investigation determined that Lisa had lied about everything she told Donna. No patient at Grady Memorial Hospital had a sister that fit Lisa's description, and "Lisa's" true identity was never revealed. Raymond's case was never solved— according to Donna because the police never had a genuine interest in the case.

"The investigators kind of brushed me off," Donna says.

Instead, law enforcement officers quickly concluded that Raymond had probably been sold to someone outside the United States. The evidence of misconduct grew stronger when Donna went to the police department a decade later to obtain a copy of the original police file documenting Raymond's disappearance. There was no file on record. Police admitted that all the evidence in the case was gone. Today, the evidence still remains unrecovered.

"With the file gone it was like Raymond never existed," Donna says.

Furthermore, Raymond's abduction never made headline news, which might otherwise have drawn the public attention's to the case and led potential witnesses to come forward. Only *The Atlanta Constitution* ran a brief story about Raymond's disappearance and the supposed abductor, who was last seen (according to the paper) leaving Donna's home wearing a blue head scarf to apparently cover up scars on her temple. There was no further information.

"I was poor and black. No one had an interest in my story, and I did not know what to do, other than pray," Donna says.

THE ATLANTA CHILD MURDERS

After Raymond's kidnapping, Donna struggled to get by on her own because no one in her family had the resources to help her. Especially not after the family lost a second newborn child a month after Raymond's disappearance: Mike had died from sudden infant death syndrome.

"I had no support from my family," Donna says. "Missing a baby was new to all of us, and no one knew what to do. I was a teenager and needed someone to be there for me, telling me what to do, but I had no one. I had to get through by myself. My way of doing so was checking out emotionally. It was all too much to handle. I became numb towards everything." Donna explains that she went through therapy; still, she has never fully recovered from the trauma of losing Raymond. The difficulty she has had in regaining her emotional comportment is perhaps due to having to cope not only with the grief of losing a baby in the years after Raymond's abduction, but also with others' criticism. Donna even felt that her boyfriend, Raymond Green, and other relatives blamed her for her son's disappearance.

"If I cried they said I was losing it, and if I was acting strong they said I did not care about my baby. Such accusations are very hard to deal with when you are only sixteen years old," Donna notes.

During the course of the following months, Donna lost trust in everyone. Even her boyfriend. When he wanted to take their firstborn child, Raymonda, to see his mother, Donna did not trust that he was going to bring Raymonda back home. Her mistrust resulted in many conflicts with Raymond; shortly after, the couple split up. Donna was now completely on her own, which led to even further isolation and emotional distress.

Less than a year after Raymond's disappearance two other children went missing in Atlanta. Alfred Evans was thirteen years old and Edward Smith was fourteen years old. Both boys were found dead in a wooded area; their bodies were discovered just four days apart. These two murders were the beginning of what would soon be known as the Atlanta Child Murders.

Over a period of two years twenty-nine people were abducted and killed. At least two dozen of the victims were black children between the ages of seven and seventeen. The racial profile of the victims led the police to investigate whether the Ku Klux Klan was responsible for the crimes. Given the number of victims, media coverage of the Atlanta Child Murders quickly brought about national awareness of the crimes. Frank Sinatra, Sammy Davis Jr., and The Jacksons performed at benefit concerts to raise money for the victims' families, and CBS produced "The Atlanta Child Murders", a miniseries about the slayings starring Morgan Freeman and Martin Sheen.

Despite the enormous attention the murders received, police were never able to convict anyone of the murders, even when they finally had a prime suspect in custody. In 1982, a twenty-three-year-old man was arrested and later convicted for murdering two people who were not among the victims of the Atlanta Child Murders. Law enforcement could not prove the convicted murderer was also responsible for the other twenty-nine murders that took place from 1979 to 1981.

Because Raymond had been abducted just eight months before Alfred Evans and Edward Smith were found, the police investigated whether Raymond's kidnapping might also be related to the other cases, but a connection was never established.

"It was a really scary time in Atlanta," Donna recalls. "But I was so numb to it all, and I really did not fear Raymond had been killed. I had the sense that if I started fearing for his life I was gonna end up in a place I could never get out of again," she says.

Two years later, Raymond's case was investigated in relation to another abduction. In 1981, Louise Lett was charged with the kidnapping of Shanta Yvette Alexander, who was snatched from Grady Hospital, just as Raymond had been taken. When police arrested the woman she had a two-year-old boy in her house. Police tried to determine if the boy could be Raymond, but a footprint test proved he was not. However, people later speculated that Raymond might have been the victim of a group of criminals who specialised in abducting babies from Grady Hospital. An investigation later revealed that seven babies who all had a link to the hospital were kidnapped between 1978 and 1996. All of the babies were black, and they were all kidnapped by women. One of those babies, in addition to Raymond, has never been found.

Although the investigation of the similarities between the case of Shanta Yvette Alexander and Raymond was inconclusive, Donna slowly recovered from years of shock and suffering. As she regained her emotional strength she intensified her focus on what had happened to Raymond and who the abductor, "Lisa", really was.

"I never found out, but whoever she is, she is a woman with mental problems. Otherwise she would not be capable of stealing another person's child. My main concern has always been if she was able to take care of Raymond and give him a good life. I pray for her in order to forgive her and move on, but besides that I do not think about her anymore. She is not worthy of my thoughts," Donna says.

Donna's healing began in earnest when she got in touch with a group called Team Hope. The group is made up of ordinary people who one day were forced to live every parent's worst nightmare: the trauma of having a child go missing or be exploited.

WILL NEVER RECOVER

Donna says that through Team Hope's network, she has met with hundreds of parents in the same situation as herself. And it is through those parents' willingness to share their stories that Donna has realised she is not alone with her sadness and pain.

"It gives me hope and comfort knowing I now have the support of others, and that many [parents have] reacted the same way as I did when Raymond went missing," Donna explains.

Knowing the importance of having others' support, Donna often voluntarily gets in touch with parents whose child has recently been abducted. Donna wants to help these parents understand that although they are now feeling an unbelievable pain and going through the worst uncertainty possible there is still a way forward.

"Having a missing child touches every corner of your being, and the traumatic event takes you to the core of who you are," Donna says. "But I tell others that they can make it, because I am the living proof they can."

However, Donna believes that parents of missing kids will never fully recover from the traumas associated with losing a child. More than forty years after Raymond's disappearance, Donna herself still suffers.

"I have forgiven myself and accepted that I was naive and ignorant to the cruelty of the world when he was taken, but there are still times where I just break down and can't believe what happened. It just comes as a flood, and I sink really deep. When it happens, I just try to believe and pray," Donna explains.

Even though today, if he is alive, Raymond would be a grown man in his forties, Donna still sees him as her little baby, and she misses him every day, wondering if he now has his own children.

"Hopefully, he lives somewhere with his own family, not knowing that he was abducted as a child. But it is painful not knowing how he is and where he is. He could be living next door and he could be across waters, sold to a family in another country. The uncertainty is the worst," Donna notes.

Even though she accepts that Raymond could be living on a different continent—as police speculated during the years following his abduction—Donna has never given up looking for him. A few years ago, she thought she had finally found him after a man reached out to her from Germany.

The only details the man knew about his own background were that he had immigrated to Europe from the United States in the late 1970s, and that at the age of eleven he was abandoned by the woman he had until then believed to be his mother. After reading Donna's story he contacted her, and the two began communicating by letter and phone. Together they spoke about the missing link they both felt in their lives. Eventually they decided to have their DNA tested; they waited for the test results for months. When the results came back, there wasn't a match. But as a result of the great absences they share, the two have established a bond for life.

"I had a feeling he was Raymond, and that my son was coming home. When I found out it was not him, I was devastated, and I mourned for days. But then I started believing again. I had to make sure that I was not gonna get stuck because of the disappointment. If I get stuck I cannot move forward—and I have to keep searching for Raymond," Donna says. She adds that she also once had a tip about a man who had been sold out of the United States to a group of people in Belize. The man was now an adult searching for his natural mother. He also matched Raymond's profile…until the DNA test again showed differently.

In spite of her disappointments, Donna has not given up. Today, she has DNA samples in databases around the world, in the hopes that one day someone's DNA will be a match with hers.

While waiting to be reunited with Raymond, Donna finds comfort watching the news about other missing children.

"Constantly I see stories about children that have been gone for years and years. Suddenly they make their way home," Donna says.

Like many other parents who have lost children, Donna also has found comfort in religion. She notes that she is a spiritual person, and that she has accepted her fate because it is by God's choice.

"Parents of missing kids become spiritual—because if not, how are we gonna get through the pain? We need someone to go and trust in. We have to go to our Maker so he can make it right," Donna explains.

The mother especially turns to God when the worst of thoughts appears. At times she still cannot help wondering if Raymond was raped, if he has been tortured or killed. However, at the end of the day, she has chosen to believe he is in a good place.

"Because I know God has the whole world in his hands; and in the hands of God, that is where Raymond and I are still united," Donna says.

Faith has also given her the strength to get through a second tragedy that happened too early in her life: Her husband, Raymond Green, died at the age of thirty-five, after suffering from an aneurysm. Donna had gotten back together with Raymond after a twelve-year separation. Old love never dies, as she says. Instead, love had resulted in her marriage to Raymond, and the birth of another five children with him.

"My husband's death was another great loss, but there was nothing I could do," Donna says. "When tragedies happen you have to take your inner cup and fill it up with something new. All this hurt and disappointments I had to put in a place, and that was God's place. He took my tragedy and led me to help others who are in the same situation."

A REAL PHOTO

Despite the tragedies Donna has experienced she refuses to turn bitter or to be adversely affected by events she has no power to change. She explains that we all have to accept that at different stages in our lives, tragedies will happen to each of us. And with Donna having experienced more tragedies than most people, she can be a positive light in other people's darkness.

"You just have to wake up every day and take one step. The next day you will take two steps. Other times you'll get knocked down, but you always have to get up and believe again. Then suddenly you take three steps." Donna notes that this approach to life has gotten her through her darkest times.

Over the years she has also managed to turn the pain she has experienced in life into professionally helping others. She has worked as a drug counselor for teenagers, but the most important counseling she offers is to other parents who have been deprived of their children due to crimes against them. She offers that support through a small organisation called the Raymond Green International Outreach of Hope, which she founded a decade ago. The organisation's mission is outlined in a few words on its website:

> *Each year, thousands of children go missing. The pain and anguish felt by loved ones is immeasurable! Every second, every year, and each decade that a loved one is missing is devastating. The Raymond Green International Outreach of Hope specializes in cold cases, and offers support to those who feel forgotten.*

On the days when Donna feels forgotten and doubts if she can get through them, she reminds herself:

"If I give up who's gonna look for Raymond then?"

Donna has also spent a lot of time trying to help her other children deal with the trauma of Raymond's abduction. The oldest of her children is forty-one years old, and the youngest are twins, twenty-one years old; but even though five of Raymond's siblings were born after Raymond went missing, they are all affected by the crime that was committed. The entire family suffers, distrusting others.

"Some of Raymond's siblings have been very watchful towards their children, because they know what happened to their brother, leading to them being overprotective with their children. Just like I have always been with mine, and still am, even though they are all grown now," Donna says.

Together with her children, Donna honours her missing son once a year, when families, friends, and advocates hold an annual remembrance for Raymond. Often, up to one hundred people come out to honour him. The event gives Donna the chance to keep Raymond's story alive. Because a breakthrough in Raymond's case might one day come about through other people's interest in his story.

"Everywhere I go I tell my story, because someone might hear it and suddenly remember something that will bring Raymond back. I am sure that one day the story on the news will be about Raymond coming home to me," the mother says.

When Donna tells her story she often brings her picture frame with the drawing that portrays how Raymond might look today based on facial characteristics of his siblings. The drawing has been made by certified forensic artist Diana Trepkov, who uses cognitive memory interview techniques to help create composite sketches. The two women met almost ten years ago to create the first sketch of Raymond. For six hours the forensic artist interviewed Donna about what happened on the day Raymond was taken. Donna just poured out details about everything from what the weather had been like, to what the air had smelled like, to specific features of both Raymond and the abductor. The details led Diane Trepkov to create two sketches—one of Raymond and one of the kidnapper. When Donna saw the image of "Lisa" she was aggravated.

"It felt like I was face to face with the woman who kidnapped my baby," Donna says.

However, she was pleased by the drawing of Raymond, which Diane created using age-progression techniques to show how he might look at the time Donna met with the forensic artist. Donna hopes one day to replace the drawing with an actual photograph of her son.

6

LONG-TERM MISSING

Almost all missing children in the United States make it back home alive. Of all children reported missing, as many as 99 percent return home. In regards to abduction cases specifically, nine out of ten recoveries are made within three days of the abduction; almost half of the recoveries are made within three hours.

The cases that take the longest to solve are family abduction cases. In these cases, an average of 326 days passes before an abducted child is returned home.

Even though an overwhelming majority of abduction cases are resolved relatively quickly, one percent of all abductions do not have a happy ending. In some cases law enforcement and parents search for the missing children for years—and at times, even decades—investigating every lead but without recovering the missing child.

Janis McCall has been searching for her daughter, **Stacy,** for almost three decades.

A GRADUATION GIRL GONE

Missing: Stacy Kathleen McCall
Date of Birth: 04/23/1974
Missing From: Springfield, Missouri
Missing Since: 06/07/1992 (18 years old)
Classification: Endangered Missing
Interview: Janis McCall, mother of Stacy

Janis had been looking for her pink slippers for weeks. Every inch of the house was searched again and again, but the eye-catching footwear was nowhere to be found. Then one morning Janis woke up and the slippers were next to her bed, as if they had been there the whole time.

Janis was puzzled. She could not understand how the slippers had ended up right in front her. But this was not the first time something odd had happened in the house. Once, Janis had been reading a book—and suddenly it was gone. In that case, too, she had searched in vain…and then one day the book was lying right in front of her on the kitchen counter.

The inexplicable events did not upset Janis. She soon came to a conclusion regarding who had found the slippers and the book for her.

"It was Stacy's way of showing that she cared about me, and that she did not want me to worry about things," Janis explains.

At times the mother had also felt her daughter's physical presence while she went about with her daily routines. One day, Janis was preparing dinner…and when she turned around she caught a glimpse of Stacy sitting in the wooden chair, where she always used to relax before going to school. That particular afternoon she was sitting watching her mom cooking—but as soon as Janis felt her daughter's presence, she was gone again.

"Sometimes her spirit shows up. When it happens I always feel her right here next to me. I just wish it would happen more often," Janis says, knowing that she can never expect to see her daughter again in real life. Because only one person knows where Stacy has been for the last twenty-six years. The person who took her.

Therefore, Janis clings to the memories she has of her daughter… and she remembers the last time she saw Stacy as if it were yesterday.

Stacy was eighteen years old and had just graduated from Kickapoo High School in Springfield, Missouri. That afternoon, Janis felt proud when her daughter walked out the front door, heading for a graduation party. She was wearing a yellow shirt, flowered bikini pants, and a fourteen-inch gold herringbone chain necklace. On her fingers she wore two rings: a flat gold initial ring and a ring with a small diamond. However, one of her most distinguishing characteristics was her long, dark-blonde hair that always flowed down below her waist.

When Stacy left the house that afternoon Janis never imagined that a few days later she would find herself printing missing persons posters—posters that displayed her daughter with various lengths and colours of hair.

"We went to a salon where they changed her hair [in the original portrait] into different styles and colours so we could put out posters with different photos of her. We wanted people to be able to recognise her even if she was forced to change her looks. I will never forget how hard it was putting my daughter's picture on those missing persons posters. Once I did, reality sank in. Stacy was gone," Janis says.

When Stacy went to the graduation party she met her friend, Suzie Streeter, who was a year older. The girls decided to spend the night at a motel in Branson, Missouri, to give them an early start in the morning, when they planned to visit the White Water amusement park.

Janis did not like the plan. She was worried that the girls would get involved in a car accident while driving for almost an hour to Branson at night. She was therefore thrilled when Stacy called at ten thirty P.M. to tell her mother they had changed their plans. They would stay in Battlefield and sleep at a friend's place, where they were also celebrating their graduation.

"I was so relieved they were not driving at night," Janis remembers, "but had I only known....When I told Stacy 'I love you' and said goodbye, I never imagined it was the last time I would speak to her and hear her voice."

The party at the friend's house ended abruptly when the police showed up after receiving a complaint of loud noise coming from the house. The girls decided to leave.

Today, Janis wishes Stacy and Suzie had gone straight to Branson, no matter how dangerous driving in traffic at night would have been, because sometime after the two teenagers went back to Suzie's mother's house to get some sleep before heading out the next morning, the worst nightmare a parent could ever imagine became a reality.

"We don't know what happened in the house, only that the two girls disappeared without a trace. For twenty-six years we have lived not knowing if our daughter is dead, if she is being held captive, or if she is living a life far away, brainwashed by the person or persons who took her," Janis says.

One thing is for certain though. On June 7, 1992, a crime took place at the Streeter house on East Delmar Street sometime after two a.m., after the girls had arrived at the home.

Later that morning, when the girls failed to show up for their ride to the amusement park, two friends went to the Streeters' house to see if Stacy and Suzie had overslept. But Janelle and her boyfriend, Mike, had not even gotten to the front door before they felt something was wrong.

THE MESSAGE

The lampshade over the porch light was broken and shattered all across the floor. Three cars were parked in front of the house, but no one answered the door when Janelle and Mike knocked.

The cars belonged to Stacy, Suzie, and Suzie's mother, Sherill. Janelle and Mike realised it was unlikely that the girls would have gone to the park without using at least one of the cars.

The friends decided to enter through the unlocked door. They called out for the girls, but they were met only by the family's Yorkshire terrier, Cinnamon. The dog appeared anxious, to the point where Janelle believed it wanted to be held in her arms. She picked the dog up, and it calmed down.

While the friends searched the house they noticed that the blinds in Suzie's room had been bent as though someone had tried to look through them to peer out onto the driveway. They found Sherill's reading glasses in her room, next to an open book. It seemed as if Suzie's mother had been interrupted in the middle of the night, while she was reading.

When they continued their search, Janelle and Mike grew even more confused as to why Stacy, Suzie, and Sherill were not in the house: all of their personal belongings *were* there.

Stacy's clothes were neatly folded next to Suzie's bed. The friends found three purses lined up next to each other on the stairs, all untouched. Later, investigators discovered that Sherill had almost $900 in her purse that she was apparently going to deposit in the bank. Law enforcement quickly concluded that whatever had happened in the house, it was not a robbery that had gone wrong. There were no signs of a struggle.

"If a crime had taken place the girls would have been taken by surprise in their sleep, or they would have been the victims of someone able to subdue three women," Janis says. "One thing is sure, if Stacy had the chance, she would have fought back."

None of the friends thought a crime had been committed. Instead, they decided to wait for the girls to return and offer a logical explanation for their disappearance. While waiting the friends decided to be helpful.

They quickly grabbed a broom and swept up the glass on the porch. They also turned off the television that was on when they had first walked into the house. Strangely, however, it was set on a station that wasn't available.

Then, suddenly, the phone rang.

When Janelle answered the phone she heard a man's voice. The caller refused to identify himself, he just whispered foul words that were of a sexual nature. The verbiage was so unpleasant that Janelle immediately hung up.

Meanwhile Janis was trying to get in touch with her daughter. She did not have Sherill and Suzie's phone number on her, but when she finally tracked it down she left three messages for Stacy. Late that afternoon, when her daughter still hadn't replied, Janis decided to go to the house.

"I knew something was dead wrong when I found out Stacy's clothes were still there," Janis recalls. "Stacy would never go out in just her underwear and expose herself. But I did not want to admit to myself that something might have happened. Instead I tried to find relief in the fact that all the cars were still there."

When she got to the house on Delmar Street that afternoon Janis did not listen to the messages on Sherill's answering machine. If she had, she would have realised that her voice was not the only one on the machine—there was a man's voice as well. He had chosen not to identify himself, as someone who later listened to the messages reported. And because the messages were of a sexual and rude nature, the person who listened to the messages also deleted them, making it impossible for the police to follow any traces of the vocal tracks when friends of the three missing women later told investigators about the calls.

Janis stayed at the house throughout the evening together with Janelle and Mike, hoping that Stacy would come back, though the feeling that something was wrong constantly grew. So many things did not add up, big and small details alike. Like the fact that Sherill's cigarettes were still in the house when everyone knew she never went anywhere without them. Sherill was a chain-smoker, and her son, Bartt, later said that his mother would not even leave her bedroom to go into the living room to give him a message without bringing her cigarettes. She *always* took them. It seemed more and more unlikely that the three women would have left of their own free will.

"It was a very stressful night," Janis remembers. "We just sat and waited for a sign. Slowly I started to realise that perhaps Stacy had been at the wrong place at the wrong time. Stacy and Suzie used to be good friends, but over the years they lost contact. More or less they spent the night together by coincidence, because they went to the same graduation party. Stacy was probably taken by whoever had already planned on taking Suzie or Sherill," Janis suggests.

However, because it seemed so unlikely that someone had actually vanished without a trace no one called 911 until late that night.

"If I had called 911 earlier I would have admitted that we had an emergency situation. I didn't want that. I just wanted to keep the hope of them walking unharmed through that door alive," Janis says.

But she could not help starting to fear that a movie she and Stacy had watched three nights earlier might now become her reality. The movie was about Adam John Walsh, who was abducted in 1991 from a mall in Hollywood, Florida. Adam was six years old, and he had gone to the mall with his mother. While she did her shopping, the son asked permission to watch some older boys play video games in a nearby store. When the mother returned ten minutes later, Adam was gone. The older boys had been causing trouble, and a security guard had asked them to leave. Authorities believe that Adam followed the boys outside the mall, as he did not want to be alone. When the older boys left he was probably kidnapped.

A couple of weeks after Adam disappeared, his severed head was discovered by two fishermen in a canal one hundred miles from the mall. The rest of Adam's body was never found. Two years later his fatal story was told in the movie *Adam*.

"I cried and cried when we watched that movie, saying I could never handle going through the experience of having a child abducted. Then at the age of forty-five, I was," Janis explains.

GRAVE ROBBING

The police were alerted, but investigators did not have many leads. Many people had entered the house while waiting for the women to come back, and the crime scene was contaminated. Even the broken glass on the porch, which could have contained DNA evidence, was useless: It now lay in the Dumpster across the street. Investigators were forced to look for leads in other ways. They found one on Suzie's shelf. A book about Satanism.

When investigators began digging deeper and looked over their files of past arrests, they realised that Suzie had previously been dating a guy who had been arrested for being part of a grave-robbing gang.

"It turned out they had broken in to a mausoleum and taken the gold teeth out of some skulls," Janis says.

Suzie had been so disgusted by her boyfriend's actions that she broke up with him. And when officers interrogated Suzie regarding her ex-boyfriend's arrest, she agreed to testify against him at the upcoming trial. Now friends started to speculate whether Suzie was "disappeared" so she couldn't testify.

"But police could not prove the boyfriend had anything to do with the girl's disappearance, and he was cleared," Janis explains.

The mother was questioned by the police the day after her daughter went missing. But she was so shaken by the situation that she almost missed her appointment at the police station.

"I have gone by the police station a thousand times. I knew exactly where it was, but that morning I just could not find it. I drove around the police station twice without realising I was already there. Everything was so stirred up that I could not think straight," Janis says.

It didn't help that investigators had asked Janis to bring her daughter's dental card. Janis figured that this request meant they suspected something serious might have happened, namely, the death of Stacy.

But once Janis was in the interrogation room her coolness returned. A female officer asked Janis all sorts of questions, and the mother was happy to answer. Several investigators were listening to her responses in another room.

"I gave them so much information, and I told them so many personal things about Stacy, because I wanted the investigators to feel that they knew the person they were searching for. I wanted it to be personal," Janis explains.

She was not the only one giving the investigators information. A couple of weeks after Stacy, Suzie, and Sherill vanished, another woman came forward. She told police that on the morning of the women's disappearance she had seen Suzie drive an avocado-coloured Dodge "panel" van. Suzie had looked scared while driving the vehicle, the woman said. The woman also reported that she had even heard a man screaming threats at Suzie from the back seat.

Still, months passed without any significant leads coming in; but Janis and her husband, Stuart, were not going to give up. They continually handed out posters with Stacy's picture. They created billboards. At the same time, Janis did numerous interviews with both local and national media. The family frequently called the media themselves to ask for interviews, because Janis knew it was important to keep the women's disappearance at the top of people's minds.

"I also knew it was important not to cry on TV. I was afraid it would be turned around and used on Stacy if she was watching us… and if she should get upset with seeing me crying, that might aggravate her kidnapper and get him aggressive," Janis explains. "Every time we were being interviewed we felt we were talking directly to Stacy and to her kidnapper. We were saying to Stacy that we loved her and would never give up and we were saying to the kidnapper that we needed Stacy back in our lives."

While the police conducted their investigation the McCall family conducted their own investigation as well. Stacy's father and a couple of friends went to search a house where the missing daughter was rumored to be. Not because they did not believe in law enforcement, but because the family simply wanted to do anything they could to get their daughter back if she was trapped nearby.

"My husband almost got himself killed when they went around looking for her, because not everyone appreciated what they were doing and instead they got aggressive," Janis recalls.

The family's search always proved to be in vain, but after a few months Janis felt they might be getting a step closer to knowing who the kidnapper might be. The police unexpectedly received a tip from the family of a woman named Sharon Zellers. The family was living in Florida.

Miss Zellers was killed when she was just nineteen years old. She had been on her way home from work when she was murdered. The teenager was found a few hundred feet from a hotel where a young man, Robert Craig Cox, was celebrating with his parents. Robert had just graduated from his army training.

During the night the young soldier had gone out on his own, but when he returned to the hotel he was covered in blood. When his parents rushed him to the hospital he told the staff that he had bitten off a part of his tongue. However, the examiner quickly concluded that was impossible due to the direction of the bite. Therefore, someone else must have bit it off. As Miss Zellers' deceased body was found at about the same time, police decided to interrogate Robert Craig Cox. He denied any involvement, and because DNA testing was not reliable in 1978, the soldier walked without being charged.

Shortly afterwards, Robert Craig Cox travelled with his army unit to California, where he served as a highly skilled Army Ranger—until he was arrested in 1985 for the abduction of two women on two separate occasions.

TELL THE TRUTH

Once in custody Robert Craig Cox was transferred to Florida and indicted for the murder of Sharon Zeller. This time the ex-soldier was found guilty and placed on death row, but the sentence was later reversed because of a lack of DNA evidence.

Instead of ending his days on death row, Robert Craig Cox served only seven years for the abductions in California. After being released on parole, he moved to Springfield, Missouri, to live with his parents.

In Missouri he searched for a new beginning and work. He found a job at a car dealership—the very same place where Stacy's father worked as a salesman, and where he may very well have met Stacy.

"She was the kind of girl that would make people's head turn. It's very likely Robert Craig Cox would have noticed her," Janis says.

When this information became public, people began speculating whether Stacy had been his prey all along, and if he perhaps had followed her on the night she disappeared. And with his background as a Special Forces soldier, he had the skills to subdue three women.

A few years later Robert Craig Cox sparked additional speculation about his involvement when he conducted an interview with the Springfield television reporter, Dennis Graves. The interview was conducted while Robert Craig Cox was still in prison; it aired the first time in 1996 on KYTV in Springfield and again in 2017 on the national television show *True Crime Daily*.

When the convicted criminal was asked about Stacy, Suzie, and Sherill, he told the reporter, cryptically, "I just know that they are dead. That is not my theory. I just know."

However, once law enforcement's attention had shifted to Robert Craig Cox, investigators found they were not able to charge him with the crimes related to Stacy's, Suzie's, and Sherill's disappearances, because the prisoner's girlfriend provided an alibi for him, stating that he had been with her at church when the women went missing.

But when Robert Craig Cox was later arrested and put in jail in Texas for aggravated robbery, his ex-girlfriend finally came forward, admitting that Robert Craig Cox had never been with her on the night of the abductions.

"Apparently, Robert Craig Cox had instructed her to give him an alibi, so we do not know the truth about his whereabouts on the night [in question]," Janis says.

During the interview for *True Crime Daily*, Robert Craig Cox also stated that he might one day tell the truth about what happened on that horrible night in 1992. He is prepared to tell all he knows once his eighty-two-year-old mother is dead.

"It is not a nice thing, but I am just waiting for his mother to pass away," Janis says. "I want to know if Robert Craig Cox is toying with us, if he just wants the attention, or if he actually knows what happened to them."

When asked, Janis says she believes that Robert Craig Cox is the kidnapper, and if she gets the chance she will go to the prison where Robert Craig Cox is incarcerated to confront him. Today, he is serving a life sentence in Texas for aggravated robbery.

"It does not matter if the police are there or not. I want to go and see him and let him know what he has done to us. If he took them I want him to see how much he has hurt us. He not only did the crime to them. He also did it to us," Janis explains.

She would also like to confront Robert Craig Cox in order to find her daughter's remains. If he was responsible for her death he would know where Stacy has been buried. Janis says she just wants to bring home what is left of her daughter.

"If I can't see him in prison, I hope he is reading this book so he knows about the discomfort and pain we feel. Hopefully that would make him feel so sorry that he tells exactly what he did and how we can [get] Stacy's remains back. I would want him to know that we won't pursue the death penalty. We just want answers. If she is buried, if she is in a lake, or if she is still alive," Janis says.

Although she believes Robert Craig Cox abducted the three women, she still refuses to pronounce Stacy dead; she won't do that until her remains have been found. For several reasons. Janis says she could be wrong about Robert Craig Cox, and she still hopes that Stacy is living safely somewhere in the world, and that one day she will return home.

"In my mind I know the chances of her coming back are almost non-existing, and if she comes back she is not gonna be the same person, but that does not matter. I just want her back, and I will have her any way she is," the mother explains.

Janis also says that is why she still does interviews about her daughter.

"I hope she sits somewhere reading this book too, and if she does she will know that we would like her to come back. She can come by herself, with kids, or anyway she likes. I think it could still be a possibility that she has been brainwashed and lives somewhere believing that her life was intended to be this way though she is being held hostage, but if she reads this perhaps she will recognise who she was and decide to come home. We would be so happy if she does," Janis says. She also explains that hope never leaves her, even though she has lived almost three decades without any trace of Stacy.

At times Janis believes that she has seen her daughter in the streets. When she gets that feeling she always walks up to the woman to find out if she might be her daughter. Often, the woman thinks Janis is a bit crazy, but she doesn't care.

"It is painful thinking I have seen her and then realising I was wrong, but what if I was right? Today it does not happen often, but [near] the beginning of her disappearance I often thought I saw her. But the pain that always follows when I realise I haven't has, over the years, gotten too hard to bear," Janis confides.

GO TO HELL

When Janis is asked to talk about how she has managed to keep her hopes up for twenty-six years, she answers very quickly: "God." Janis is a religious woman. When she realised there was nothing she could do to change what happened to Stacy, "I turned it over to God," she explains.

"If Satan is there and makes people do wrong, God is still there to forgive and give people the chance to do right," she says. "But if this person that might have killed the girls is dead I would not want him to be there in heaven with them. I would want him to go to hell. It is terrible to feel this way, but that is how I do feel. He has ruined so many lives and done [so] much evil. He should pay for that," Janis avers.

However, she no longer has the same need for revenge that she did during the first several years following Stacy's disappearance. Back then she would have picked up a gun and shot the perpetrator right away if she had had the chance. That is how angry and hurt she felt.

"But I do not have that need anymore," she says. "Especially my grandchildren have changed me. They have brought a new love into my life. I am very attached to them, and I do not want them to think I am a bad person."

In the beginning when her daughter went missing Janis always contemplated what she had done wrong. Today she no longer blames herself. Instead she feels that the abduction of her daughter is the kind of injustice that happens to innocent people and that you cannot prepare yourself for, especially if you are the victim of someone's vicious acts. You just have to accept that tragedy may be a part of life that nobody wants. According to Janis the best way to move on is to stay positive and never give up hope.

"Because the only ones responsible are the people who commit these crimes. And they do not deserve also to be ruining the lives of the relatives," Janis says.

She still hopes that her daughter's abductor and possible killer will one day face justice in a court of a law. Janis no longer needs to know exactly what happened to her daughter on that summer night in 1992. Because reality might be too cruel to handle.

"I can't stand thinking about what Stacy has gone through and might still go through. What Stacy, Suzie, and Sherill have felt and perhaps still feel," Janis says, adding that she sometimes even has dreams about the pain her daughter has suffered.

"In my first dream after her abduction she was sitting on a wooden chair with her hands behind her back, and she just said, 'Help me'. That is my typical kind of dream. I have also dreamt she has been killed. When I wake up it is difficult carrying on," Janis acknowledges.

Over the years, Janis has forced herself not to speculate about answers she cannot provide for herself. Today, the most important thing for Janis is simply knowing whether her daughter is alive or dead—and, in the worst case scenario, where her remains are.

"I feel Stacy is always here with me, and that I can talk to her. But I think that all parents who have lost a child need their remains and a physical place where they can go and talk to them. It gives you comfort having them present. And I want that headstone of hers for all of us so we can find peace," Janis says.

Until then Janis finds another kind of comfort by helping other parents who have had a child be abducted. After Stacy's disappearance Janis founded an organisation called One Missing Link. Through the organisation she has helped thousands of desperate parents over a period of twenty years. She has always given them the same advice that she has lived by for the past twenty-six years: take one hour at a time, then one day at a time.

"And days became weeks, months, years—and now decades. But I have always had the feeling that if I can make it through today, I can make it through tomorrow as well," Janis observes.

Due to several health issues, Janis had to close down the organisation, but some parents still call when they lose a child. As Janis listens to their stories they always brings back bad memories of her own, but she would never say "no" to helping others, because she knows from her own experience that parents missing a child need to talk with others to get through their grief.

"From my story I have been able to help people and tell them what comes next, right after an abduction. How they will react during holidays, what situations are especially rough. I can also tell them what to do to get through these situations. The most important thing is always talking to others about the persons they are missing," Janis notes.

According to her, parents get comfort knowing that God is taking care of their loved ones, no matter where they may be.

"That gives me comfort as well. But I do wish He instead would send her back home," Janis confides.

missingkids.org

MISSING
HELP BRING ME HOME

Alexandria Lowitzer

Missing Since:	Apr 26, 2010
Missing From:	Spring, TX
DOB:	Feb 3, 1994
Age Now:	25
Sex:	Female
Race:	White
Hair Color:	Brown
Eye Color:	Blue
Height:	5'2"
Weight:	145 lbs

Alexandria's photo is shown age-progressed to 19 years. The
went missing. Alexandria's ears and nose are pierced. When
teeth and her hair was dyed dark red. Alexandria may go by

DON'T HESITATE! ANYONE HAVING INFORMATION SHOULD CONTAC

CALL 911 OR
1-800-8435678 (1-800-THE-LOST®)

Harris County Sheriff's Office (Texas) 1-713-

Follow us twitter.com/missingkids facebook.c

(Missing person flyer provided by Jo Ann Lowitzer)

Survivor, Alicia Kozakiewicz (private photo by Alicia Kozakiewicz)

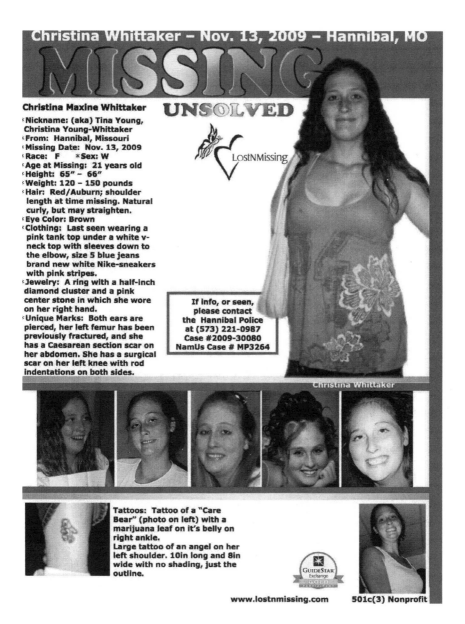

Christina Whittaker – Nov. 13, 2009 – Hannibal, MO

MISSING

UNSOLVED

Christina Maxine Whittaker

- Nickname: (aka) Tina Young, Christina Young-Whittaker
- From: Hannibal, Missouri
- Missing Date: Nov. 13, 2009
- Race: F   *Sex: W
- Age at Missing: 21 years old
- Height: 65" – 66"
- Weight: 120 – 150 pounds
- Hair: Red/Auburn; shoulder length at time missing. Natural curly, but may straighten.
- Eye Color: Brown
- Clothing: Last seen wearing a pink tank top under a white v-neck top with sleeves down to the elbow, size 5 blue jeans brand new white Nike-sneakers with pink stripes.
- Jewelry: A ring with a half-inch diamond cluster and a pink center stone in which she wore on her right hand.
- Unique Marks: Both ears are pierced, her left femur has been previously fractured, and she has a Caesarean section scar on her abdomen. She has a surgical scar on her left knee with rod indentations on both sides.

If info, or seen, please contact the Hannibal Police at (573) 221-0987
Case #2009-30080
NamUs Case # MP3264

Christina Whittaker

Tattoos: Tattoo of a "Care Bear" (photo on left) with a marijuana leaf on it's belly on right ankle.
Large tattoo of an angel on her left shoulder. 10in long and 8in wide with no shading, just the outline.

www.lostnmissing.com   501c(3) Nonprofit

(Missing person flyer provided by Cindy Young)

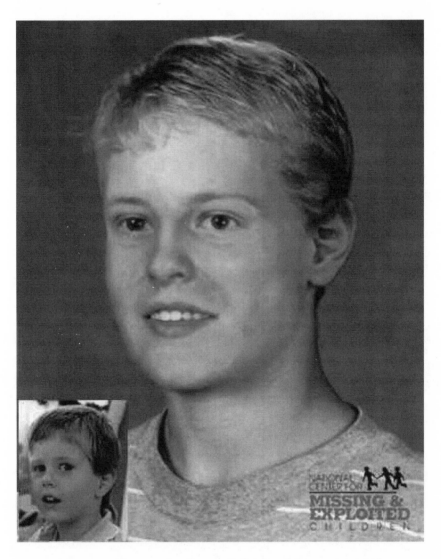

Missing, Christopher Louis Zaharias (photo provided
by Louis Zaharias)

Missing, Lisa Mae Zaharias (photo provided by Louis Zaharias)

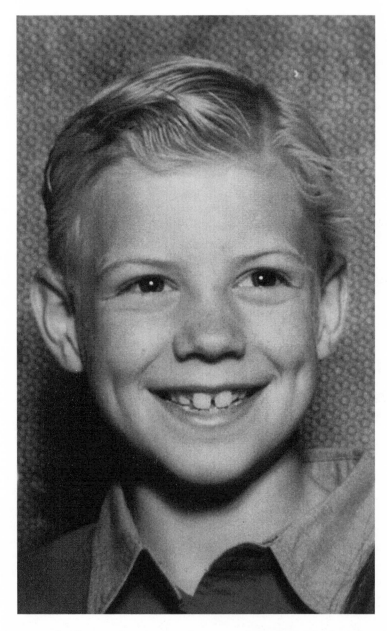

Deceased, Christopher Meyer (private photo by Mika Moulton)

Deceased, Johnia Berry (private photo by Joan Berry)

Survivor, Alicia Kozakiewicz and her mother Mary Kozakiewicz
(private photo by Alicia Kozakiewicz)

(Missing person flyer provided by Marianne Asher-Chapman)

Missing, Raymond Green (photo provided by Donna Green)

Deceased, Samantha Runnion (private photo by Erin Runnion)

Missing, Stacy McCall and her mother Janis McCall
(private photo by Janis McCall)

Survivor, Rhonda Stapley (private photo by Rhonda Stapley)

7

THE MOST LIKELY VICTIM

The majority of children and adolescents who become victims of non-family abductions are girls between the ages of twelve and seventeen. Almost eight of ten victims of non-family abductions are females, a study from the U.S. Department of Justice shows. During the course of the study, authorities investigated 105 abduction cases that occurred over a one-year period. Nearly two-thirds of the victims were white and one-third were black.

When law enforcement investigated the cases they found that one-third of those abducted were taken from a place where they were living or staying. Another one-third were abducted at the kidnapper's house. The final third (36 percent) were taken from a public place.

When an adolescent is taken, most of the time the perpetrator's approach has incorporated deception or nonthreatening behaviour.

In almost two-thirds of the abduction cases studied by the Department of Justice, the victims voluntarily went with the kidnappers—at first. Young children often go voluntarily with the perpetrator.

In most cases, regardless of the child's age, the victim is lured into—and transported from the abduction site by—a car.

Six out of ten victims of non-family abductions are detained for more than twenty-four hours, and two-thirds of the victims are sexually assaulted during their detainment. Thirty-five percent of the victims, who are stereotypically depicted as being the victims of only a kidnapping, are also physically assaulted by the abductor.

Jo Ann Lowitzer's daughter, **Alexandria**, was abducted when she was sixteen years old and on her way home from school. Today, almost ten years later, she is still missing.

A RUNAWAY INVESTIGATION
Missing: Alexandria "Ali" Joy Lowitzer
Date of Birth: 02/03/1994
Missing From: Spring, Texas
Missing Since: 04/26/2010 (16 years old)
Classification: Endangered Missing
Interview: Jo Ann Davis Lowitzer, mother of Ali

For weeks, Ali rushed home from school to check on the eggs in the bird's nest. Her father, John, had discovered the nest in the family's backyard during a barbecue party, and the fifth grader immediately made it her mission to check on the eggs every afternoon after school. As soon as she found them to be safe and sound she would call her mother at work to tell her.

One day Ali discovered the eggs had finally hatched, and she immediately fell in love with the newborn birds. But her joy was quickly shattered. A snake in the nest was eating the birds and there was nothing she could do to save them. She called her mother that afternoon, heartbroken. When she finally found a neighbour to come and kill the snake, it was too late. All the birds were gone. Ali felt that she had failed them, because it was in her nature to help others, whether it was people or animals who were in need of it.

"If I had let her bring home every stray dog she found there would not have been room for the rest of us in the house," Jo Ann recalls. She adds that her best memory of Ali was witnessing how she always felt compassion for others.

"She was such a caring, loyal, and happy girl," the mother says.

Even though she had an interest in other people, Ali was also very shy. Jo Ann explains how proud it made her feel when her daughter overcame her shyness and sang an unaccompanied rendition of the National Anthem at a local rodeo. Jo Ann also feels the pride she has in her daughter whenever she looks around her living room.

"My house is full of craft work. Ali was so artistic. She made art all the time and was hoping to study art at college. She was so generous and always gave her artwork to others. When I look at her art in my house it brings back so many great memories of her," Jo Ann says.

However, one memory overshadows all else.

It was a nice, warm Monday at the end of April. Ali spent the weekend at her mother's house, constantly practicing playing an acoustic guitar. The sixteen-year-old girl had recently picked up an interest in playing guitar, and she was determined to learn how to master it.

Ali put the guitar away only when her new boyfriend, DJ, came over to the house. Like other teenagers in love, Ali was over the moon with joy and excitement. When she went to school the next morning nothing indicated that her happiness was about to be shattered. After class, prior to Ali taking the school bus back home, she called her mother at work. At the time, Jo Ann was working for a shipping logistics company. Ali asked if it would be okay to walk to her workplace, the Burger Barn, on Cypresswood Road, a quarter mile from her home in Spring, Texas, just north of Houston. The sophomore was going to pick up a paycheque.

"She had never walked there before, but she talked me into letting her for the first time. That is the biggest regret in my life," Jo Ann says.

When Jo Ann returned home a couple of hours later, Ali had not yet returned. Jo Ann came to the conclusion that Ali had probably spontaneously accepted a work shift, so she decided to send her daughter a text, asking when Ali wanted Jo Ann to pick her up at work. But there was no reply from Ali.

"The first time I reached out and she did not react, I knew something was wrong. She always responded right away. But this day ten, fifteen, thirty minutes went by without a reply. Then an hour, then two hours. I tried to [give] the benefit of the doubt, but I just had this feeling that something had happened," Jo Ann recalls.

Instead of waiting at home, Jo Ann decided to drive to the restaurant. When she got there she found out it was closed.

"I just freaked out," Jo Ann remembers.

For a couple of minutes she sat in her car trying to figure out what to do before calling Ali's father, John, from whom Jo Ann had recently separated. John tried to calm down his former wife, and together they decided to wait to alert the police until they had called all Ali's friends to find out if she was with them.

"We just called everyone we could think of," Jo Ann says.

Around eleven P.M. the parents realised that no one had seen their daughter after she got off the school bus to walk to the restaurant. At that time, she was wearing a gray hooded zip-up sweatshirt, black-and-white checkered "skinny" jeans, and black sneakers. Jo Ann finally called the local police department—but their response was less urgent than what Jo Ann had been hoping for.

"I was so disappointed with the way the police reacted," Jo Ann says.

According to Jo Ann, law enforcement tried to convince her and her former husband that, given their daughter's age (sixteen), she was probably just a runaway teenager who would soon be home again. Jo Ann says the police made it very clear they would rather wait for Ali to return by herself than launch an unnecessary search; therefore, police did not issue an AMBER Alert.

"They just told me to wait for her, but I have now been waiting almost ten years for her to return," the mother says.

FAMILY FIRST

Jo Ann tried to convince the police that her daughter had been taken, because Ali's makeup, purse, clothes, money, and phone charger were still in the house—everyday stuff a runaway teenager would normally bring with them when they left. And when the family checked Ali's phone records they were even more certain a crime had been committed. Ali constantly spoke on her phone, and she sent thousands of texts every month. But ever since she got off the school bus her phone has not been used except for a text she sent ten minutes later asking her friend, Jay, to come over to her house later that afternoon.

Jo Ann says that in spite of all these facts law enforcement took several weeks before acknowledging that Ali had not run away but was more likely the victim of a crime. When the police department finally accepted this conclusion, the case was escalated to the homicide unit, with the promise of using more resources to find Ali.

Although the police were finally showing the urgency Jo Ann had been hoping for from the beginning, the escalation of the case also meant the homicide detectives now started directing their investigation towards Ali's family. Her brother Mason and the father John were both taken to the station for questioning. Jo Ann says the police kept her son in the interrogation room for hours and that they accused him of getting into an argument with Ali that escalated into a fight resulting in him killing his little sister.

"They tried to force Mason to confess. It really scared him. He was nineteen years old and just a teenager. It scarred his heart, being accused of having killed his sister. Afterwards he would not talk about it, but you could see the pain in his eyes. Today, it is still very emotional for him to talk about, because it traumatises you, being accused of having killed a person you love deeply," Jo Ann says. She describes the children as growing up in a close-knit family where the siblings were each other's best friends.

Ali constantly wanted to be with her brother. Jo Ann recalls how she would rather play with Mason's action figures than with her own Barbie dolls.

"Like all siblings they had their rivalry. 'Mom, he looked at me' or 'Mom, she's playing with my toys'. That type [of thing]. But their love for each other was so obvious and deep," Jo Ann recalls.

A few years after Ali's disappearance, Mason moved to Seattle, Washington. There were too many sad memories connected with the town of Spring, Texas.

"I still get upset when I think about how law enforcement treated this innocent young man," Jo Ann says.

Her son was not the only family member being questioned by detectives. The police department also interrogated Ali's father, John.

Before the investigators cleared him as a suspect, the father had to take a polygraph test to prove he did not kill his own daughter.

The interrogation took a toll on the entire family. Each family member not only had to prove their own innocence, but they also were forced to accept the fact that law enforcement often investigates the involvement of the victim's family's first, before considering other suspects, Jo Ann says.

"It was hard. We were under suspicion—and at the same time we felt that we were losing important time. Instead of questioning us, they should have been searching for Ali. Time is crucial in abduction cases," Jo Ann observes.

Therefore, the family decided to launch their own investigation. Ali's father, John, watched surveillance footage from the school bus company. The footage showed his five foot, two inch tall, 145-pound daughter getting off the bus then walking in the direction of Burger Barn. But security footage from a nearby gas station indicated that Ali never made it to the restaurant.

The family also hired two private investigators, who came up with different suggestions regarding what might have happened to Ali. But shortly after Ali's disappearance, one of the private investigators came across an important piece of information that brought the family closer to having an explanation regarding what might have happened to their daughter.

On the day Ali disappeared, she had ridden the school bus with an acquaintance.

"This guy had a crush on Ali, and when he invited her out on a date, she told me that she had turned him down," Jo Ann recalls.

When the young man was questioned by the private investigator Jo Ann had hired, he said he had spoken to Ali on the bus. She had problems with her cell phone, and he helped her fix it.

"That would have given him the chance to disable the phone so she could not reach out for help later," Jo Ann says, striving to find an explanation for why her daughter never replied to her texts.

Surveillance videos from the bus later showed that the young man was lying. He had never been on the bus.

The private investigator, Amber, could not prove that the teenager had anything to do with Ali's disappearance, though his story changed several times while being questioned. Still, Amber found his explanation so suspicious that she decided to continue investigating him and his family. Her findings were shocking.

"It turned out that his older brother was involved with drugs and human traffickers in the state of Ohio," Jo Ann explains. "We now feared that the little brother had been so angry with Ali rejecting him, that he had convinced his older brother to abduct her and force her into prostitution in Ohio. Amber also found out that there was a trafficking ring between Texas and Ohio," Jo Ann adds.

A MURDERER IN TOWN

Around the time Amber made her discovery about the older brother, a woman called Jo Ann from Columbus, Ohio. The woman said she had seen Ali's picture on a missing persons website, and that Ali looked similar to a girl she had recently noticed in her local community. Amber, the private investigator, traveled to Columbus to follow up on the lead. Once in Ohio she worked together with local police and undercover agents. She visited crack houses and brothels. At the same time, a cop told Amber that he had seen a girl that reminded him of Jo Ann's daughter. The girl went by the name Ali Cat. Furthermore, the police officer said that he was aware the woman was from Texas, but not that she had been reported missing. A police informant also confessed to having seen Ali: She recognised her by a scar on her forehead. The informant lead Amber to a brothel where she had claimed to have seen Ali. In the brothel Amber saw a girl who looked like Ali. However, Amber had no authority to intervene as a private investigator; instead, she alerted local law enforcement. A plan was put together, but when the police finally obtained a warrant to raid the brothel, the women who had worked there were nowhere to be found. Amber visited the brothel after the raid took place. She, too, reported that the women who had formerly worked there no longer were on the premises. She believes that the Ali look-alike had been moved to another brothel.

"Perhaps because someone tipped off human traffickers about the raid," Jo Ann explains. "At least, this is what some people suspected. I still have a percentage [of faith] left in me that believes she could still be in Columbus."

Jo Ann explains that is why she has made several trips to Ohio, 1,200 miles north of Texas, and that she will follow any tip that seems reasonable.

Following Ali's disappearance Jo Ann created a Facebook remembrance page for her daughter. The mother explains how the family often received tips about her daughter's whereabouts. The tips, she wrote in a post on Facebook in 2014, came "from everywhere. Alaska, San Diego, all the way to Miami and everywhere in between (and some of them at the same time)." In the same Facebook post, she described why she specifically followed up on the tip indicating Ali was seen in Ohio:

For me this one just seemed a little different so we decided to travel to Ohio to investigate deeper. While there we did not find the girl everyone was saying was Ali. But a few months after...Columbus police did arrest two different girls they believed to be my Ali. Both of these girls were lookalikes and one of them has been identified as the girl everyone was seeing.

To this day we continue to get leads of people seeing Ali in different states. And we continue to follow those leads. Ali is still missing and her whereabouts still unknown. We do not know why she was taken or by whom. But I continue to hold onto hope that she is still alive out there and that we will find her. I will never give up my search to find you. I miss you bunches.

Besides investigating whether Ali became a victim of human trafficking, Jo Ann has watched other leads develop. Two years after Ali's disappearance, a man named Brandon Lavergne confessed to killing two women in Louisiana. Brandon had relatives in Spring, Texas, whom he had been visiting around the time Ali went missing. He had earlier been a suspect in the case. When Ali's disappearance was made public a witness reported to the police that he had seen a man try to lure Ali into his white truck near the Burger Barn. The witness had even managed to grab a few numbers off the truck's licence plate. When the police checked the numbers they discovered that they matched part of the plate on Brandon Lavergne's car, which was later discovered burned about fifty miles from Spring. The police questioned Brandon Lavergne about his involvement in Ali's disappearance, but a former employer provided him with an alibi. Law enforcement was never able to prove he had any connection to the case.

No matter what might have happened to Ali, Jo Ann says she can't imagine what Ali might have been going through. But if she were to be given a chance to decide her daughter's fate, she says, without hesitation:

"I have rationalised that she could be forced into prostitution; and the other scenario is that she is being held hostage in a basement somewhere. I know it sounds bad, but of these two possibilities I hope she would be forced into prostitution. I see that as [the] lesser evil," Jo Ann explains.

However, there is another possibility, an outcome that Jo Ann will not accept.

"I admit, I struggle a lot with if I believe she is alive or not. Until there is a body I am gonna believe that she is still alive. And until she is found one way or another I am gonna keep searching," Jo Ann notes.

Although Ali's disappearance adversely affects Jo Ann's life in so many ways, she still tries to turn her pain into knowledge and wisdom that others can benefit from. Today, Jo Ann has accepted there is nothing she can do to change her daughter's destiny; instead, she can enlighten other parents about the dangers that certain parts of our society can pose to their children.

"My eyes have been opened to this epidemic of missing people that we are facing in America. I just wish I had become aware of this earlier. There are so many parents going through this nightmare every day. Earlier I just closed my eyes and followed others. But today I am so much stronger, thanks to Ali. Now I speak my mind, and I seize every opportunity to put [the public's] focus on this problem," Jo Ann explains.

EXPLOITED BY OTHERS

One way to put the focus on what Jo Ann calls "this epidemic of missing people" is by constantly encouraging parents to tell the story of their missing children. Another way is to constantly remind authorities that they have a responsibility to both prevent and solve these abductions.

To remind society of its responsibility, Jo Ann tried for years to make Texan lawmakers adopt a resolution to recognise April 26, the day Ali went missing, as "Texas Missing Persons Day." Finally, in 2017, lawmakers did.

"At times I feel I can conquer the world," Jo Ann proclaims. "And at times I feel that if I had the chance to capture the person responsible for Ali's abduction I would end up in prison with him because of what I would do to him. I am no longer a bystander in my own life. Today I stand up and act—unfortunately on a sad background."

Besides dealing with the worries and pain resulting from her daughter's abduction, Jo Ann also has to deal with the ruthlessness of other people. Jo Ann still receives many tips about her daughter's whereabouts, but some of the tips simply reveal how cruel certain people can be.

"Over the years I have received numerous messages from people claiming to know where Ali is, but they will not tell [me] until I pay them thousands of dollars. We have experienced so much exploitation from other people who try to benefit from our daughter's disappearance. It happens to a lot of families who are missing their children," Jo Ann says.

She has reported most attempts to exploit her daughter's disappearance to law enforcement. Meanwhile, in times of sorrow and pain she finds comfort in her family and ex-husband. The couple was separated at the time of their daughter's disappearance, but they both still support each other and are the best of friends.

"We have always been a team when it came to the kids. We have always been there for each other. [Near] the beginning of her disappearance John was the driving force when it came to the search groups. He was the strong one. But a year after her disappearance he began to take things a lot harder. When I asked him for follow-ups on tips he had no answers, because he no longer had the strength to follow up. He put so much into it, and then the sorrow caught up with him. Today the roles are reversed. Now he comes to me for follow-ups," Jo Ann says, emphasising that ten years after Ali's abduction the entire family still is struggling from the consequences of the crime.

For Jo Ann, the most difficult part is not knowing whether Ali is still alive. But she often feels her daughter's presence.

Jo Ann still lives in the same house in Spring, Texas, in case Ali returns home. And the mother always keeps the door to her daughter's old bedroom open. At times Jo Ann gets the feeling that her daughter is sitting on the bed, drawing, just like she used to.

"Other times," Jo Ann reveals, "I dream of her. I have a dream where I am in a public place, and then I see Ali sit at a different table with friends. In the dream I just walk up to her and ask where she has been and if she is all right," the mother explains.

Another way Jo Ann finds she can feel a connection with Ali is by writing her poems. Jo Ann posts the poems on Facebook. At other times she makes crafts, just as Ali always did.

"I think of Ali while doing it. And I give a lot of craft[s] to other families. When I do, I feel I create something beautiful for others, just like Ali always did," Jo Anns says. She adds that she will continue hoping that one day Ali will be back home to do crafts with her, just like she used to.

"Today, Ali is twenty-five years old, and she still has life ahead of her. She often expressed her desire to have her own family. I hope that one day that wish will come true. I can't give up that hope, because I want Ali to keep believing in it no matter where she is. And I will forever be looking for my daughter and not her body," Jo Ann says.

8
PROFILE OF AN ABDUCTOR

The National Center for Missing and Exploited Children has analysed a decade of attempted abductions and related incidents committed by individuals unknown to the victimised child. The incidents involved more than 9,800 children; they were committed by 9,027 perpetrators.

The analyses showed that 96 percent of the perpetrators were men whose average age was 36. In almost nine out of ten of the cases studied, the perpetrator worked alone. The children included in the study tended to be older when they were victimised by a male perpetrator, in comparison to incidents involving female perpetrators; the latter tended to victimise infants and toddlers.

Over the years law enforcement has become more aware of who the perpetrators of child abductions tend to be. Police have generally intensified the fight to prevent abductions and, of no less importance, their hunt for the kidnappers. In 2006, the FBI created the Child Abduction Response Deployment task force, also known as the CARD team. According to the FBI the team "works to recover victims as quickly as possible and helps apprehend those responsible for taking them".

The team consists of more than sixty agents and can be on the scene within one or two hours after the crime has taken place. The team establishes on-site command posts to centralise investigative efforts, working hand in hand with state and local law enforcement agencies. The CARD team also helps identify registered sex offenders in the area, coordinate forensic resources, and incorporate the FBI's technical assets, "which play an increasingly larger role in investigations where every minute counts", as the bureau describes it.

Over the years technological advances have also made it easier for police to apprehend abductors within the first crucial hours of an abduction—the period of time when children are often killed. When it comes to long-term abduction and unsolved homicide cases, the FBI also employs offender profiling techniques. When Marietta Jaeger's daughter, **Susie,** was abducted by a serial killer, the FBI used her disappearance to create the first profile of child abductors anywhere in the United States.

A KISS GOODBYE

Missing: Susie Jaeger
Date of Birth: 04/19/1966
Missing from: Missouri Headwaters State Park, Montana
Missing since: 06/25/1973 (7 years old)
Classification: Endangered Missing
Interview: Marietta Jaeger, mother of Susie

A cool breeze awoke Heidi. Confused, she looked around and realised that the cold came from a big hole cut in the tent. She quickly went from surprised to scared when she discovered that her little sister Susie, who had been lying next to her, was missing.

Heidi rushed through the night to a nearby caravan where her parents were sleeping.

"Wake up, wake up!" she screamed.

Marietta tried to calm down her upset daughter, explaining that she was sure the youngest of her five children had merely gone to the bathroom; but when the mother saw the hole that had been sliced in the tent, her confusion turned to fear. When she found the two stuffed lambs that Susie always slept with in the grass a few feet away, she had no doubt regarding what had taken place.

"I knew it was real and that Susie was not just wandering around. Clearly, something terrible had happened. I just prayed that someone had not taken her," Marietta says about the moment when she realised that her seven-year-old daughter had been abducted.

The Jaeger family had arrived at Missouri Headwaters State Park in Montana three nights earlier, after driving for a week through eight states after leaving their home in Michigan.

For the next month, Bill and Marietta Jaeger were going to spend what they hoped to be a once-in-a-lifetime dream vacation that they would talk about for the rest of their lives.

"When we got there, I was just so happy. I felt I could not have been blessed with a better life than the one I had. Our trip had turned out to be the best time our family had ever had together. But the dream soon became a nightmare," Marietta says.

The mother awoke all the kids and told them that Susie was gone while her husband drove off to find a phone and call the police. Shortly after 4:00 a.m., the dispatcher received the call at the sheriff's department in Gallatin County.

In the beginning, officers thought Marietta's worries were a false alarm, as the area was known to be quiet and safe. But when the investigators saw the hole in the tent, they also began to worry. A violent crime had taken place, and FBI agents from the Bozeman field office quickly joined the search for the missing girl.

There were only a few clues at the campsite. Among them were footprints that investigators found in the morning dew of the grass.

The footprints led to a nearby parking area, but the driver of the vehicle the prints apparently led to had taken off. Soon, one of the biggest missing persons searches in Montana was launched. A few hours later, the park was swarming with officers and members of the National Guard searching for the missing girl from horseback, helicopters, and boats.

While searching Missouri Headwaters State Park, some of the officers had a flashback to five years earlier when they had been combing through the same scenic landscape, searching for evidence in another case. During an outing of a troop of Boy Scouts, a twelve-year-old boy was stabbed and beaten to death in the middle of the night while he was sleeping in a tent. Police never solved the case; now, the investigators worried that the killer was back.

The FBI and local authorities immediately set up a command post next to the Jaeger family's caravan while searching the area with Marietta as an onlooker.

"There were helicopters in the air, and they also searched the nearby river. Every time the boat stopped, my heart stopped. I was so scared that they were gonna pull up the net and that Susie would be in it," Marietta says.

Meanwhile, hundreds of citizens called in with tips—and police investigated all of them. One of the callers was a man who urged police to investigate his twenty-four-year-old neighbour whom he described as acting weird and showing an unusual interest in his children. Police knew the neighbour, but when they investigated David Meirhofer, nothing seemed suspicious, and when another call came in, it changed the investigators' focus.

One week after the kidnapping, a man called a deputy sheriff at home. The man claimed to be the kidnapper, and he demanded $50,000 in ransom; the money, he demanded, was to be delivered to a bus station. To confirm that he was not a prank caller, the kidnapper described a minor deformity on the missing girl's index fingers.

"When Susie was taken, I had to describe every little detail of her body to the FBI. Every little mark and every little scar, but we had over the years gotten so used to her most unique feature, the index fingers, that I completely forgot to mention it to the investigators. Therefore, nobody knew of them, and I immediately knew he was the kidnapper. He could not have obtained these facts from any documents, but only by looking at my little girl," Marietta notes.

SITTING BY THE PHONE

The call gave the mother hope. Perhaps the kidnapper was only interested in money, and perhaps Susie would be back just as suddenly as she had disappeared. The Jaeger family did not have the ransom money, but a rich man heard of the case and offered to deposit the money with the FBI, saying he was happy if his money could help save the girl's life. Everything was in place for Susie's safe return. Marietta waited impatiently for the kidnapper to call back with details about when he wanted the drop-off to take place.

"We waited and waited and waited, but he never called back. It just tore me up. I was so frustrated, and there was this particular day that was so hard to get through. I could see my other children were suffering. We all were. When I went to bed that night, I said to my husband, that even if the kidnapper came back with Susie alive, I could still kill him with my bare hands and a smile on my face," Marietta says.

Despite her anger, she refused to give up hope. She was going to stay faithful to Susie and continue to believe her daughter was alive and that the investigators would soon find her. After spending a month in the state park, the family had to return to Michigan. The FBI was ending the ground search, and Marietta had to take care of her other four children and get them back to school.

"For a month, we had watched, waited, and worried while law enforcements officers searched the area," Marietta explains. "But leaving was extremely hard because it was the last place I had seen Susie and it felt like I was now leaving her behind—all by herself with her kidnapper."

Before leaving, the Jaeger family said goodbye to the many local citizens who showed up at the campsite every morning to feed the Jaegers, and to pray for Susie's safe return.

"I came with five children, but I had to leave with four," Marietta explains.

The family also said goodbye to the federal agent, Pete Dunham, who previously told Marietta how crucial it is to find a missing person within the first forty-eight hours.

After a month of searching, the agent was sure that Susie would never be reunited with her family. Still, he could not tell Marietta that all the agents believed Susie was dead.

Instead, the agents were eager to catch the kidnapper. They installed recording devices on the Jaeger's phone in case the kidnapper called back.

"I was always sitting by the phone waiting for him to call. Only one time did I leave the house, as I had to pick up my son from school. During the ten minutes I was gone, the kidnapper called," Marietta says.

Her eldest son, sixteen-year-old Dan, picked up the phone. On the other end, a voice asked if he would like to see Susie again.

Dan immediately turned on the tape recorder and asked the kidnapper to release Susie, but the kidnapper replied that he could not. He said that he still had her and that he wanted to exchange her for the ransom, but since the FBI had gotten involved, it was difficult for him to release Susie without getting caught. He would need more time to figure out a way of getting Susie back to the family.

"Seconds later, I walked in the door, and I could tell right away from the look on Dan's face that he had just spoken to the kidnapper," Marietta remembers.

Immediately, Marietta notified the FBI, and the bureau tracked the call to a pay phone at a diner in Wyoming. When local police officers showed up, the caller was long gone; but the call did not change the agents' opinion. From their experience with previous cases, they still believed Susie was dead and that the kidnapper called merely to torment the Jaeger family. But Marietta and her family never gave up hope. Instead, the family printed thousands of posters that they sent to sheriff departments all over Montana and the neighbouring states.

Still, there were no leads. The sheriff's department in Gallatin County changed its focus after receiving another disturbing call eight months after Susie's kidnapping.

This time, a worried mother called. Her nineteen-year-old daughter, Sandra Smallegan, disappeared from her home in Manhattan, Montana—a small town with approximately 1,500 inhabitants just ten miles from the campsite where Susie had been abducted.

Sandra Smallegan was last seen when she returned to her apartment around midnight after hanging out with friends. The next day, she and her car were gone, and police opened another missing persons case in what used to be a peaceful rural area of Montana.

The police searched for the car to find a lead. Officers drove to the most remote places hoping to find evidence...and at the end of a dirt road, they would find some. When an officer stopped outside an abandoned ranch, he found a pair of women's panties. Immediately, he entered the barn, as he feared the young woman was trapped inside. Instead of finding the missing person, he found Sandra Smallegan's car, covered by a tarpaulin.

PROFILE OF A KILLER

Investigators sealed off the ranch and nearby fields where they found the gruesome remains from a murder. More than 1,200 bone fragments were spread out over an area of seventy-five yards. The bones had been chopped and burned before being dispersed, but by matching the results of forensic analysis to dental records provided to the investigators, authorities determined that the bones belonged to Sandra Smallegan.

"I could not help worrying if Susie had suffered the same," Marietta confides.

FBI investigators feared that the same person was guilty of both crimes. The investigators worked closely with local authorities. Often, the investigators met for lunch at a local diner, where they shared information. A young man often sat nearby, trying to listen in. He also often approached the investigators, directly asking them about the two cases. The officers knew the man.

David Meirhofer spent three years as a U.S. marine before returning to Manhattan, Montana, where he worked as a building contractor. The young man had previously been questioned by police in the case of Susie's disappearance, when the neighbour had mentioned him to investigators. Now, David Meirhofer once again attracted attention, because the investigators knew that if a person showed interest in a particular case, he often had something to do with it.

Investigators decided to look into David Meirhofer once again, and it turned out that he had previously dated Sandra Smallegan. Agents brought him in for questioning and asked him to undergo a polygraph test. David agreed to the polygraph, but denied to having committed the crimes. When he passed the polygraph, the police had to let him go, and investigators were once again left with no clues or suspects in either of the two cases.

Instead, local FBI agents continued to work closely with colleagues at the FBI Academy in Quantico, Virginia. The investigators from Quantico had recently developed a new method of identifying murderers. The method was called offender profiling.

When employing offender profiling, a profiler tries to determine certain characteristics of the unknown offender by studying evidence at the scene of the crime and the behavioural patterns of the kidnapper as indicated by that evidence. The abduction of Susie was the first time the FBI used this new method.

The profiler in Sandra's and Susie's cases suggested that because of the stealthy manner of the abductions and the way the victims must have been under surveillance prior to their kidnapping, the perpetrator probably had military training. The profiler also concluded that he was probably a schizophrenic.

Once again, the name of ex-Marine David Meirhofer came up. If he was a schizophrenic, he would have been able to lie without showing any stress and thereby pass the polygraph test.

The profiler also made another prediction. He was sure that the kidnapper had become so personally involved in his crime and the lives of the victim's family that he would call the Jaeger family on the anniversary of Susie's abduction to celebrate his crime like normal people would celebrate a work anniversary.

The day before the one-year anniversary of her daughter's abduction, Marietta Jaeger did an interview with a newspaper in Montana. In the interview, she said that she hoped the kidnapper would call again and that she felt sorry for him. Perhaps this would trigger him to call and taunt her.

One year after Susie vanished, the call came in the middle of the night at the exact minute of the kidnapping.

"He asked if he was speaking to Susie's mom. When I confirmed [that he was], he said 'I am the guy who took her from you,'" Marietta recounts.

And then, he just hung up. The call had been too short for the FBI to track it and for Susie to get any information out of the kidnapper—but then the unlikely happened. The phone rang again.

"I just listened to him. He needed to tell me that he was the one in control. He just needed to taunt me and to get me hysterical. So, I let him," Marietta says.

For several minutes, she listened patiently to her daughter's kidnapper bragging about his vicious deeds. He even said that Susie now considered him family, and that they were travelling together all the time, enjoying life. He also said that as he was speaking to Marietta, her daughter was sleeping in a room next to him. He would not let Marietta speak to her, but her mother went along with it: She asked him what size shoes Susie wore now, how he was educating her, and what she liked doing.

"I knew it was important to keep him on the phone so the FBI could track the call. So, I just started talking to him. Slowly, I took control of the conversation. I told him I was praying for him, and I asked if I could do anything to make his life better. That made him break down. He sobbed and he sobbed and he sobbed and all of a sudden, he said: *'I wish this burden could be lifted off me.'* I could not get him to elaborate about what he meant by *burden*, but that was the closest he came to admitting that he had killed Susie. An FBI agent later said that the goodness in me overcame the evil within him," Marietta says.

For more than eighty minutes, she spoke to her daughter's kidnapper. Marietta hoped it was long enough for the FBI to track him—and they did. All the way to a relay station in Florida. But a system failure there prevented the agents to track the call any further.

One month later, the call unexpectedly exposed the kidnapper.

A ranch owner in Montana complained to the telephone company that someone had tapped into his phone and made a long-distance call to Michigan—to the home of the Jaegers.

The ranch owner had a suspicion about who could have tapped into the phone line. A former employee at the ranch had been a communication expert in the Navy and would, therefore, know how to tap the lines. The former employee was David Meirhofer.

The police compared the voice that was recorded during the conversation with Marietta with a recording the police made when they had previously brought Meirhofer in for questioning right after Susie's disappearance. The FBI had a match.

MET THE KIDNAPPER

When confronted by police, David Meirhofer refused to admit to being the kidnapper. Instead, he named relatives whose voices sounded just like his, claiming one of them might be the killer. The police arranged a "voice lineup": they would all call Marietta Jaeger one by one and repeat the exact same words the caller had used when calling Marietta on the anniversary night of Susie's abduction.

Marietta had no doubt when she identified caller number 2, David Meirhofer, as the person she had talked to that night. Her identification was considered circumstantial evidence, and after a new interrogation, the suspect passed a truth serum test. The investigators realised they needed a confession before they could arrest him. Once again, they had to let him go.

"On his way home from the truth serum test, he tried to abduct another child from a girl scout campout; the kids woke up and scared him away, but the kids saw the back of him, and they were able to identify his clothing. It was the exact same clothing he had worn during the truth serum test. From that moment on, we knew we were dealing with a very, very sick person that presented a huge danger to all kids in the area," Marietta says.

Law enforcement knew they had to get David Meirhofer off the streets, but they still did not believe they had enough concrete evidence to obtain a conviction, and the FBI agents felt there was only one person who could get a confession out of him—Marietta.

The FBI assumed that having the suspect meet the mother would throw him off track; so agents convinced Marietta to fly out to Montana to meet him.

"I was grateful for the opportunity. I wanted to look him in the eyes and tell him face to face that I forgive him," Marietta remembers.

The two met in the office of David Meirhofer's attorney.

"The minute I saw him, I knew he kidnapped Susie," Marietta says.

For an hour, they spoke. Marietta told him to his face that she knew he had taken her daughter, but even though she tried to get a confession out of him, David Meirhofer would not crack. Instead, he proclaimed his innocence and said that he would like to help search for

Susie. After an hour, the attorney insisted that the meeting come to an end, but Marietta had difficulties saying goodbye to the man that she was sure kidnapped her daughter. So, when they shook hands to say goodbye, she found it hard to let go again, because David was now her only connection to Susie.

"When I looked in his eyes, I not only saw Susie's kidnapper. I also saw a mentally ill man. His pupils were completely black, like he was psychotic. I genuinely felt for him, just like I had the first time we spoke on the phone. That moment, I knew that my forgiveness had become a reality in my heart," Marietta says.

During her stay in Montana, she met with David Meirhofer three times; but every time was in vain. Seeing David made Marietta realise that she was probably never going to have her daughter back, so when she returned to Michigan, she packed up Susie's clothes and gave them away. She knew inside, Susie was never going to wear the clothes again.

After the futile meetings, the police had no other option than to put David Meirhofer under twenty-four-hour surveillance. They did not hide the fact that they were watching him, as they hoped their surveillance would prevent him from trying to abduct more children; but one day, he succeeded in eluding their surveillance. Police searched for him without results…until another call came in.

Exactly one year after David Meirhofer had called the Jaeger household the first time and spoken to Marietta's son, a man called and identified himself as Mr. Travis, but Marietta quickly replied:

"David, stop playing games with us. I recognise your voice."

Still, the man insisted he was Mr. Travis, and he wanted to prove that Susie was still alive by putting her on the phone. Next, a child spoke to Marietta, saying:

"He's a nice man, mommy, I am sitting on his lap."

Marietta knew the girl on the phone wasn't Susie, as her daughter never called her "mommy," but always "momma." Instead, Marietta started fearing that David had kidnapped another child and he was now holding her hostage.

"I could hear it was not Susie on the phone, and I was terrified that he was gonna take this little unknown girl's life, too," Marietta explains.

Despite her fear, she kept David on the phone by asking him questions, and she continued to call him David. Every time, he protested, and eventually he became so angry that he slammed down the phone. But before he did, he mentioned details that proved he was David Meirhofer. The information had been shared between only the two of them when they had met one week earlier at his attorney's office in Montana. When he realised what he had done, he screamed that Marietta would never again see her daughter alive.

The call came from a motel room in Salt Lake City, but when police knocked down the door, the kidnapper was long gone. Later that same day, David Meirhofer returned to his home in Manhattan, Montana.

TIME FOR JUSTICE

When David Meirhofer pulled into the driveway, officers arrested him right away. Investigators hoped to find more evidence before doing so, but the fact that he might have kidnapped and killed the child on the phone from Salt Lake City left the police with no other options.

The police never found the girl, but they were still in luck. When David Meirhofer was arrested, police found a piece of paper on him.

The paper came from the motel in Salt Lake City and had a name written on it: Travis.

Afterward, investigators searched David Meirhofer's home. They finally found indisputable evidence that he was a murderer: Body parts wrapped in butcher's paper marked with the initials of one of the victims, Sandra Smallegan.

"Right before the police arrested David, investigators called me. Forensics had determined that among Sandra Smallegan's body parts there also [was] a backbone from a little girl. I knew that was my Susie," Marietta recalls.

The authorities had a solid case. Now, it was just a matter of understanding the extent of David Meirhofer's crimes, getting a confession out of him, and finally letting a jury decide on his fate. Marietta had already made up her mind.

"He was charged with kidnapping and murder, and the penalty was the death sentence, but I had come to the conclusion that justice for Susie would not be punishing him by death, but restoration. Killing someone in Susie's name would be to violate the goodness and sweetness within her. I wanted to honour her memory, and she deserved more than her killer to be executed. Instead, I wanted the memory of Susie to be synonymous with the fact that all lives are worthy of preservation," Marietta says.

Susie's mother knew she would have something to say at David's trial, and she knew the prosecution might listen to her proposal when she requested that they would promise David a mandatory life sentence instead of the death penalty.

"In return, David was willing to confess," Marietta says.

Over the following days, Marietta and investigators were in for a gruesome confession. David would confess to four murders. His first was when he was just a teenager.

In 1967, he had been in a fight with a boy at high school. As revenge, David shot the student's thirteen-year-old brother, Bernard Poelman, when he saw the boy fishing by a lake.

The second murder happened a year later when he stabbed the Boy Scout, Michael Raney. He committed this murder to embarrass the local scouts who had earlier terminated his participation because of disciplinary problems.

Five years later, Susie would become David Meirhofer's third known victim when he was wandering the campsite and probably overheard the little girl talking to Heidi in the tent. When the girls were asleep, he cut the hole in the tent and choked her until she passed out so he could carry her away. David admitted that he had also taken Susie to the abandoned ranch, where he strangled her before dismembering her body.

Despite talking about returning Susie in exchange for ransom money a year after the kidnapping, David killed her just one and a half weeks after abducting her. According to David, he killed Susie after she became wild when he was feeling her body, as he described it to investigators, though he denied having sexually abused her.

"All this time I had been searching for her, she had been safely home in the arms of God. It comforted me knowing that for a long time she had been in a better place than the one she left. But it was painful thinking about what might have happened to her for the one and a half weeks David had her. I only found comfort in the fact it was no longer her reality," Marietta says.

Finally, David Meirhofer confessed to killing Sandra Smallegan because she would no longer date him.

According to the FBI profiler, David Meirhofer was very likely to have kept belongings of his victims as souvenirs. Thirty-one years after Sandra Smallegan's death, construction workers found her licence, wallet, and notebook when they renovated a garage in Manhattan, Montana, where David hid his "trophies" in a wall.

By 4:00 A.M. on the day he talked about the murders, David Meirhofer had given a full confession, but he would never go to trial for his crimes. At 8:00 A.M., the sheriff's wife served breakfast for him in the cell where he was being kept after giving his confession. Along with the food, she handed him a towel he could use to clean up. When they came back to collect the tray, they discovered that David had committed suicide by hanging himself with the towel in his cell.

"That was not what I wanted for David, but I had to accept his death just like I had to accept Susie's," Marietta says.

The suicide meant that authorities would not get another confession out of David Meirhofer, but they suspected him of having killed many other children in different parts of Montana. These murders happened in counties where prosecution would demand the death penalty; so David, therefore, refused to confess to these killings.

"So, because of the death penalty, these parents never had [any] legal closure," Marietta says.

After David's suicide, Marietta realized she could help another mother move on with her life.

WISH FOR REVENGE

David Meirhofer's mother was in shock when authorities revealed that her twenty-five-year-old son was a serial killer.

"She only knew him as a loving son who helped her all the time. He would clean her house, do her shopping, and pick up her prescriptions.

I tried to imagine how she was also suffering, so I decided to go and visit her. I wanted to tell [her] that I forgave her son, as I knew this would help her move on. When I visited her, we wept together as two mothers who had both lost beloved children. She became my friend," Marietta explains.

David's mom was a devout Christian. According to Marietta, people of faith often find it easier to move on in life. Marietta says that today it gives both her and David's mother comfort to know that their loved ones are with God, in a better place full of love, and that they find peace in forgiving others who have hurt their relatives. But Marietta's husband, Bill, had difficulty finding forgiveness.

"He could not let go of his hate and his wish for revenge. He ended up dying at an early age—just fifty-seven years old—because he could not deal with his feelings. He would never talk about what had happened or about our little daughter, because he never forgave himself for not being able to protect her. He became antisocial, and the hate manifested in his heart. In the end, it wore him out," Marietta says.

She says that despite David's cruel acts, she started to forgive him just two weeks after he abducted her daughter. Her forgiveness began just after she had told Bill that she was prepared to kill Susie's killer while smiling.

"Afterward, when I rolled over to go to sleep, God started wrestling with me. I decided to accept my anger, but also to deal with it. I wanted revenge for my little, defenceless girl, but I also wanted to live with dignity. I knew people who were bitter people, and they were not nice to be around. I also realised that if I became one of them, I would not be any good to my other children, so I put the ball in God's court. I said, you have to show me how to leave my revenge and how to forgive. It was a process over a long time. No matter how I felt about the person who had taken my little girl, I had to accept that though he did not behave as one, he was also God's son and just as precious to God as Susie," Marietta explains.

The mother says forgiveness was one long exercise in which she would train her heart and brain by praying for her daughter's kidnapper. She prayed that he may have good weather, that he may not have car troubles if he was out travelling, and that he may be in good health.

"And when he called after a year, I knew forgiving was no longer an exercise. I genuinely felt for him, and that is also why I never wanted the death penalty for him," Marietta says.

Before losing her daughter, Marietta was already a spiritual person. She grew up in a Catholic home, but Susie's death made her feel even closer to God. Today, Marietta feels that Susie's death gave her life a purpose.

"People say that if Marietta could forgive her daughter's killer, I can also forgive an alcoholic mother or a violent father. It gives people hope, and in that way Susie's destiny has become a gift of life to others," she explains

In 1997, Marietta cofounded Journey of Hope, an organisation that is led by murder victims' family members. The organisation conducts public education speaking tours and addresses alternatives to the death penalty.

Fighting the death penalty in Susie's name also gives her daughter a cause that is just like she was herself—a beautiful and precious little girl, Marietta says.

"God has asked me to speak against the death penalty because executions do no good for anyone. It is insulting to the victims when we execute in their name, and a law does not make the action morally right," Marietta says.

The mother explains she has worked with numerous relatives of murder victims and that she can see how cases involving the death penalty destroy everyone involved. Relatives have to wait years—sometimes decades—before they actually know what is going to happen. When the execution is actually to be carried out, it is often overturned, and the convicted prisoner receives a life sentence instead. Going through appeal cases also constantly reopens a lot of wounds, as relatives of the victims have to listen to the gruesome details of the prisoner's crime one more time. If the death penalty is actually carried out, relatives often find that they are just as unhealed after the execution as they were before.

Before God asked Marietta to speak against the death penalty, he asked her for something else.

"When I spoke to David on the phone for the first time, I felt separated from myself. God loved David through me as I listened to him and I told him that I forgave him. I really felt concern and compassion for him, like God feels compassion for all of us. And Susie was a sacrifice. God set us up and allowed this terrible crime to happen in order for me to have this story of healing to share with others, and in order for me to help this serial killer stop his killings," Marietta says.

GOODNIGHT, MOMMA

Marietta says God also spoke to her on the night Susie was abducted. Her daughter always insisted on a good hug and a kiss before she went to sleep, and on the night of the crime Susie was extraordinarily keen on getting her kiss.

"Susie was tucked away in the corner of the tent, so it was difficult reaching her, so my lips barely skimmed her cheek. But that was not good enough for Susie. She got out of her sleeping bag and crawled across her sister's so she could give me a big hug and a big kiss right smack on my mouth. *'That's how to do it, momma'*, she said, and I am so grateful for that kiss because that was the last time I saw my little girl, and I am sure this was God's way of having Susie saying not good-bye forever, but goodbye till I will see her again in a better place," the mother recalls.

Marietta says that she still has dreams in which Susie swims by her and stops to kiss her mother. It makes Marietta miss her, but she feels it is a beautiful and peaceful experience. Marietta believes it is Susie's way of telling her that they will meet again and that they are still connected in death.

"I have the comfort of knowing that Susie is not suffering. This makes it possible for me to celebrate life. I know something better awaits us," Marietta says.

Despite having made peace with Susie's death and the killer who caused her seven-year-old daughter to die, Marietta still misses and thinks about her every day.

"The pain and sorrow never leaves you when losing a child. You just have to learn how to live with it. You will always miss your child, but if you accept your loss, living becomes easier," she explains.

Marietta says she succeeded in creating a good life for herself after Susie's death, but that it has only been possible because she addressed her anger and negative feelings in order to get on with a new life based on a new reality.

"But you can love and you can be hopeful again," Marietta says.

9

THE SEX OFFENDERS

Every nine minutes, on average, a child will become the victim of a sexual assault in America. Girls are at the highest risk. One in four girls, and one in six boys, will be sexually abused before they turn eighteen years old. And most of the victims will be abused by a person they know and trust.

Every year approximately 63,000 cases of child sexual abuse are reported to Child Protective Services in the United States. Three out of ten victims are under the age of nine years old.

However, researchers estimate that only 12 percent of all cases that involve child sexual abuse are filed with law enforcement, according to the National Sexual Violence Resource Center. And it is suspected that only 5 out of every 1,000 perpetrators end up in prison.

Even though only one out of ten sexual assaults on children are committed by a complete stranger, these types of assaults are often the most dangerous. They normally do not take place in the child's home. As a victim of sexual assault, the child is also at a higher risk of being abducted and, in the worst case scenario, killed.

To protect children and other potential victims from becoming the target of sexual predators, every state in the United States has enacted laws to strengthen the country's nationwide network of registries for people who have been convicted of a criminal offense against a victim who is a minor, people who have been convicted of a sexually violent offense, or people who are deemed to be sexually violent predators.

The registries make it possible to monitor and track sex offenders after they have been released from prison. The databases provide both federal and local law enforcement, as well as the American public, information about an offender, including the offender's name, current address, and past offenses.

Although every state maintains a sex offender website, it is up to each jurisdiction to determine the specific information that it makes public on the websites.

It is a federal crime for a sex offender to not register with the appropriate authorities or to not keep his or her information up-to-date, as described in the Sex Offender Registration and Notification Act (SORNA). A sex offender typically must update where he/she lives, works, or attends school, among other information.

In several states, the requirement for sex offenders to register with the state was enacted only after sexual crimes had been committed against a child living in the state. Four months after Mika Moulton's son, **Christopher,** was abducted and sexually assaulted, Illinois created its sex offender registry. Today, Mika just wishes the registry had been created much earlier, because the perpetrator had already sexually assaulted and killed another child when he took Mika's ten-year-old son.

A FLOATING BUTTERFLY

Missing: Christopher Meyer
Date of Birth: 01/05/1985
Missing From: Aroma Park, Illinois
Missing Since: 08/07/1995 (10 years old)
Classification: Endangered Missing
Interview: Mika Moulton, mother of Christopher

Christopher loved butterflies. He spent that morning drawing a butterfly on a piece of paper. When he was done the ten-year-old boy asked his mother, Mika, to give the drawing to one of her coworkers. It was the colleague's birthday, and Christopher wanted to surprise her.

The caring behaviour was not unusual for Christopher. The boy with the cute dimples and warm smile loved making other people happy. So later that day when he looked at his mother with begging blue eyes asking her permission to go fishing at a nearby river, Mika could not resist her son's charm.

"Christopher was quite a character," Mika recalls. "He was just one of those jokesters that always knew how to get you on his side." She laughs as she recalls her son's ability to tease a "yes" from his mother.

Christopher was not only a charming and caring kid, he was also a great admirer of animals. Mika remembers how her son would always catch and release fish no matter how big they were.

"And even if he saw a dead raccoon he would stop to see if he could help it," Mika remembers.

Mika also knew she could always trust her son. If she gave him an order he would comply and live up to his words. Still, she reminded him when he left the house in Aroma Park to go play with friends at the boat launch that afternoon, that he had to be home at five o'clock for dinner. Mika therefore grew nervous when she looked at the clock on her stove: 5:22 P.M. And no sign of Christopher.

"I expected him to return any minute, but the later it got the more I started to worry. At the same time I could not help thinking that he was gonna be in trouble when he got home, because I was always very strict with house rules," Mika admits.

And Christopher knew how strict his mother could be. One week earlier, he had been out playing with friends and had lost track of time, which was unusual for Christopher. When he came home, Mika wanted to teach him the importance of keeping to the terms of an agreement. She asked her son to sit down with a piece of paper and write all the explanations he could come up with for why his mother insisted on him being home on time.

"I have never told this before, but his answer shocked me. He wrote on the paper that it was important because if he was not home on time, I might worry that someone had taken him. It was almost like he knew what was going to happen. Like he read the future and foresaw his own fate," Mika says.

Christopher was still missing by the time darkness set in, and Mika decided to go to the boat launch. Her flashlight lit her way. A police officer approached her to ask what she was doing on her own in the dark. When she explained her son was missing the officer immediately called for backup. A river and ground search was launched.

"At first people thought he drowned. I knew that could not be. The water was low and Christopher was an amazing swimmer," Mika recalls.

In the following days fire fighters, police officers, and local neighbours searched for Christopher. Everyone came out to help because Aroma Park, located seventy miles south of Chicago, was a tiny and tight-knit village. So when the news became widely known that a little boy had gone missing it concerned everyone. And Mika had no doubt that it was only a matter of time before her son would be found.

When the mother was not out looking for Christopher herself she would sit by the window in her living room, expecting him to pull into the driveway on his bike any minute.

"I could not help thinking about how embarrassed I was going to be when they found him alive and I would have to apologise to all of them for having worried about my son. On the other hand fear would also at times come creeping in on me. But then I tried to hold it down by telling myself that horrible crimes just don't happen in a small town like Aroma Park," Mika remembers.

Therefore, she also reacted promptly when Christopher's dad came to town from California with his cousin. The local police department had already asked Mika and her former husband to come down to the station to provide DNA samples. The samples would be used to help identify Christopher's body…if law enforcement ever had to. When Mika called her ex-husband's hotel room to tell him about the police department's request, the cousin picked up the phone.

"When I asked to talk to Christopher's father," Mike remembers, "the cousin just asked: 'Why, did they find his body?' Right away I just started screaming that there would be no body," Mika says.

Today, Mika says that even though she was still expecting to see Christopher coming up the driveway any time, by then most people in Aroma Park had probably realised that was not going to happen.

A few days into the search reality slowly started to sink in. Investigators asked Mika to come down to the fire station. When she arrived officers opened the door to a cargo van. Inside was Christopher's bike. It had been found in a thicket close to the river.

"But I kept saying to myself that this did not mean he was not okay," Mika concedes. "They had just found his bike—and not him. I forced myself to keep hoping he would still come home."

However, Mika's hopes were soon extinguished. Officers also showed her a shoe they had found in the river. The shoe belonged to Christopher. This discovery put Mika in a very dark spot…a place where she started to imagine the worst possible scenarios. For a while she lost her sanity, as she describes it.

"I could not hold my thoughts together," she says.

With the discovery of the bike, the shoe, a piece of Christopher's T-shirt, and a pair of Ninja Turtle underwear that was hanging in a bush near the river, people started to speculate what had happened. Mika was deeply hurt when some people suggested that she might have killed Christopher herself. They based their cruel accusation only on the fact that Mika was gay.

Mika had been married to Christopher's father, James, for seven years and had three children by him when she met a woman called Patti. The two women fell in love and were living together in the small town in the American Midwest at the time of Christopher's death. The local community was not very accepting of homosexuality, according to Mika.

"I was very hurt by [the fact] that some people could suggest we had killed Christopher just because we were gay," Mika recalls.

EYES OF EVIL

People's prejudices and the uncertainty of Christopher's whereabouts took its toll on Mika. She did not sleep for days, and she started to feel both physically and mentally stressed out. The more in despair she felt the more she also started to realise what the result of the search for her missing son might be.

"There is something in your head that does not allow you to swallow all details at once. It is too much to cope [with]. But slowly I realised what could have happened, and I promised myself that no matter what I was gonna accept the outcome," Mika says.

Eight days after Christopher disappeared Mika had to live by her promise. At three o'clock in the morning officer Jo Lynn knocked on Mika's door. For the next several hours the two women held hands as they both broke down and cried together.

Two rookie deputies had parked their squad cars early that morning and walked off into the dark. While searching for Christopher in the woods they saw a piece of plywood lying across the ground. When they lifted the wood they found a boy's corpus hidden in a shallow grave. The boy had been stabbed to death.

When the officer, Jo Lynn, conveyed the information about the discovery of the boy's body to Mika she said that investigators were not one hundred percent certain the dead boy was Christopher; but as soon as the officer conveyed this, Mika replied: "But there [are] no other children missing."

The moment Jo Lynn, according to Mika, answered "No, there isn't", the mother knew her life had changed forever, and that she was never going to awaken from the nightmare, as she describes the ordeal.

After it had been determined that the boy found by the two rookie deputies was Christopher, hundreds of people came for a candlelight vigil held outside a Methodist church in Aroma Park. Mika brought them to tears when she spoke to the crowd; according to the Associated Press, she said:

"God loaned me ten and a half years of twinkling blue eyes, dimples, and joy. It is time now to lift up Chris and ask God to use this child as our special angel."

The disappearance and death of Christopher brought back bad memories to the local community. In spite of the common belief that Kankakee County was a safe place, the community had now experienced two child murders separated by only fourteen years and five miles.

In 1981 a five-year-old girl with chubby cheeks and sandy-blond hair went missing on her way to visit friends. The other children lived just a couple of blocks down the street from the girl's home. It was a community where no one locked their doors and everybody knew each other from the barbecue parties the community frequently held.

At least they thought everyone knew everyone else.

Because Tara Sue Huffman never completed the short walk to her friend's house. Instead, she vanished without a trace.

On that warm spring day in May 1981, Tara Sue's older brother, Richard Huffman, was one of the many individuals who immediately started to search for the little girl.

Today, Richard Huffman still recalls when he passed by a certain house on the street: On the porch a boy was observing the search crew.

Richard Huffman thought there was something odd about the boy...
and he could not help looking at him. When the boys, who were peers,
made eye contact, the look in the observer's eyes shocked Richard
Huffman. He would later describe the boy as having a motionless stare.

After a while the thirteen-year-old boy suddenly stepped off the
porch and decided to help search for Tara Sue. But he had not joined
the group for long before he wandered off on his own, just as the search
team reached an old city dump. Shortly after the boy screamed:

"I found her, I found her."

When the group approached the boy, they saw he had picked up
Tara Sue's body and was holding it in his arms. In this manner Tara Sue
was found dead a few hours after she had disappeared.

Richard Huffman made eye contact with the boy again later that
afternoon when he was sitting in the back of a police car before being
taken in for questioning at the police station. Again Richard Huffman
was met by the boy's motionless, dead look. Shortly afterwards, prosecutors accused the boy, Timothy Buss, of having snatched Tara Sue
before smashing her head and leaving her lifeless body in a barrel that
he had hauled to the dump on a wagon. The teenager was also accused
of having sexually molested the little girl with a stick. Timothy Buss
was tried as an adult and convicted of murdering Tara Sue by use of
blunt force trauma.

Later, law enforcement officers recounted how shocked they
were when they realised that the boy showed no emotions while he
was sentenced to spend twenty-five years in prison. However, the
convicted murderer was released on parole after serving twelve years
of his sentence. Only a few members of the local community, however,
knew of the killer's early release from prison. As a result of Timothy
Buss being freed, Richard Huffman's gaze once again met the cold,
numb eyes of the killer.

Witnesses had told investigators that when Christopher went missing from the boat launch, he had been talking to a man. One of the witnesses was a fourteen-year-old boy who had been approached by the same man. The boy told police that the man had explained he had been raised in Aroma Park but that he recently had been living and fishing in Florida before returning to his hometown. During the conversation the boy noticed that the man had a filet knife with lures; the boy described the knife as being too big to be used for fishing. And the witness was also able to provide the police with a good description of the man. The suspect had dark hair, a distinctive moustache, and other distinguishing characteristics that would help law enforcement construct a composite sketch. When it was completed, the sketch was distributed by the local media, and when Richard Huffman opened his newspaper to read about Christopher's disappearance he could hardly believe what he saw. He was once again looking directly into the characteristic eyes of the person who had killed his sister fourteen years earlier.

"It was like he had become Freddy Krueger of Kankakee County," Richard Huffman later told the television show *Shattered* in an episode that aired on October 24, 2018.

NO GOODBYE

Investigators could not believe what they heard when Richard Huffman showed up at the police station to tell the officers they were looking for a predator who had already taken a child's life. None of them knew that Timothy Buss had been released on parole—and that he had moved back to Kankakee County—until they called the Department of

Corrections. Once they found out that Timothy Buss had been released, law enforcement immediately put a watch on him while investigating his whereabouts around the time Christopher went missing.

"But after they started following him," Mika reports, "they saw that he was trying to approach another child. And law enforcement decided to intervene."

Officers approached Timothy Buss while he was fishing along the same section of river that Christopher had disappeared from. When he was confronted, the ex-convict snapped at the officers and asked whether they were going to come question him every time a child went missing. But at the same time he did not mind cooperating when officers asked if they could search his car. He voluntarily signed a waiver letting them do so.

Meanwhile the local media was following the case closely. A missing child in Kankakee County was a big story. For her part, Mika always hoped the coverage would lead to her son's recovery. But one day Christopher was no longer the most noteworthy news.

"On Sunday morning the [main] story was that Jerry Garcia from Grateful Dead had died. I just got so angry when I found out they had pushed Christopher's story down. If there is no progress in the search for a missing child, media and people lose interest. But I could not accept that. We were talking about my little boy. He was missing and in danger, and I just thought, how dare you run another story before telling people about Christopher?" Mika recalls.

However, Christopher's disappearance would again lead the news when law enforcement revealed that the trunk of Timothy Buss' car had been found to be full of blood, and that officers had even managed to collect hair samples from the trunk. DNA testing quickly revealed a match. Christopher had been held hostage in the trunk while bleeding to death. Timothy Buss was once again charged by Kankakee County authorities—this time, with sexual assault and the murder of a child.

After the discovery of Christopher's dead body the people of Aroma Park honoured the murdered child by putting up blue ribbons around town and tying bows to trees, mailboxes, and lampposts. At the same time rage against Christopher's killer grew.

"Some [people] literally wanted to kill him," Mika recalls, "and when he was arrested police did not do a normal physical line up. Instead, they made a video arrangement [that is, a montage] at the courthouse, probably because they were afraid someone was gonna try to kill him."

While some citizens in Kankakee County wanted to harm the accused, other people speculated about what had driven Timothy Buss to kill two innocent children. Some stated that his evil had been awakened fourteen years earlier, when, one month prior to the murder of Tara Sue, his mother told her kids that she wanted nothing to do with them. But Mika did not care about that. She just wanted justice for her son, and to see him one final time.

When Christopher was found his body underwent an autopsy before being brought to the funeral home. Mika met with the home's director. After discussing the burial of her son, Mika asked to see Christopher and to say goodbye. But the funeral director refused to let her.

"He explained that Christopher had been laying outside in the summer heat for eight days, and that there was not much left of him to see. The funeral director could not let that be the last look and memory I would have of Christopher," Mika explains.

The last time Mika saw Christopher was therefore when he picked up his fishing equipment and headed to the boat launch. Today, Mika clearly recalls how she told him to be home by five P.M. However, there is something she does not remember—something very important—and that has been haunting her for nearly twenty-five years.

"I don't know for sure if he knew how much I loved him. I just wish I could remember if I also told him that when he left to go playing," Mika says.

People's love for Christopher, however, was undoubtedly on display when he was buried. At the funeral Mika's coworker—the one who had received the drawing Christopher made for her birthday—asked permission to say a few words. Peg told how affected she had been by Christopher's gesture, and she described Christopher as a butterfly that was now free to fly and play.

When the funeral procession walked out of the church and made its way to Christopher's grave, Mika was struck by a beautiful sight. A big butterfly started to float around the graveside as her son was laid to rest. Mika was not in doubt: this was Christopher's way of saying goodbye. And when the mother returned to the graveside a week later, a butterfly alighted on the grave. Mika tried to brush the butterfly away, but it would not move.

"I ended up stroking it," Mika recalls, "and when I went back to my car it followed me. It was like Christopher was saying, 'Hey Mom, it's all okay'. Today, I can still go up to a butterfly, put my fingers underneath [it], and it will just sit. I believe missing children send signs to their parents. I believe that children are much closer to angels than we are as adults," Mika asserts.

However, she met no angels while she followed Timothy Buss' trial in court. At times the description of what the killer had done to her son was so brutal that Mika had to leave the courtroom. This was especially true when she learned that her son had been stabbed more than forty times, and that he had defensive wounds on his hands and arms.

"I became so angry when I heard about how he had been fighting for his life," Mika recalls.

When she was driving home from court that day, she was still angry. But then something happened.

"I went straight to Christopher's grave. I suddenly realised he had listened and learnt from when I always told him and his siblings that if anyone attacked them they should scream, scratch, and kick while fighting for their lives. And Christopher had done so. I went to his grave to tell how proud I was of him," the mother says.

After Christopher's death Mika would often go to the cemetery. One day she went there even after it had closed. An officer approached her to tell her she would have to leave, but when he saw who it was he told her she could stay. Before he left, the officer gave Mika an important message. While he pointed at Mika's heart he reminded her that Christopher was not lying dead in his grave, he was still alive inside of her.

"And it is true. Christopher will forever be a part of my soul," Mika says.

However, carrying on with life has not been easy for any of Christopher's relatives.

Christopher's grandfather worked as a barber not far from Aroma Park, but none of the customers knew of his relation to the murdered boy. Customers would therefore sometimes come into the barbershop and talk about the crime that had upset the entire county. Christopher's grandfather would not say anything as he listened to them. He just tried to cope with his grief.

"But some time after the funeral he suddenly said we could not stay victims, because then the killer would win, and we definitely did not want that monster to win," Mika recalls. She also describes how the murder of Christopher affected his siblings, especially the sister, Cari, who today is thirty-eight years old. She has been deeply affected by Christopher's death. Mika says that she has never managed to fully restore the relationship she had with her daughter before they lost Christopher.

"My daughter is hurt and torn from what happened," she says. "She has lived through all of this as well. At the same time she just wanted to be anonymous and go on with her life. She did not want to always be seen as Christopher's sister. She wants to be herself," Mika concludes.

Cari was hurt by her brother's death in other ways. Mika explains that there is often so much focus on a missing or deceased child that siblings feel ignored and not as important to the parents as the lost child. The sibling's feeling of neglect can easily turn into anger.

"I love all my children very much, but I understand that especially my daughter had the feeling that my love for Christopher was much deeper than the love I had for her. Because all focus is often on the missing child, and many siblings suffer from what is called 'left behind sibling syndrome'. It was not till my daughter was an adult [that] I found out how she had suffered from me putting all my attention on Christopher, and because I was always talking about him. It was heartbreaking finding out that she thought I felt more for Christopher than her," Mika explains.

She also admits that as a grandmother she has been very affected by her son's death. Mika describes herself as being overprotective of the family's youngest members—at times to an extent her own daughter has not appreciated.

"She does not want to live with the same fear for her kids as I have for my grandkids. But with the experience I have gone through, I cannot help being very protective," Mika says.

She adds that since Christopher's death there has always been a certain landmark in her life. Her youngest child, Cameron, who is twenty-six years old today, was only two years old at the time of Christopher's death.

"When he lived to become eleven years old, I was so relieved," Mika confides. "I have also felt this relief when my grandchildren have turned eleven years old. Because then they have all made it further in life than Christopher did." She says there is only one grief that has been harder than her own.

"That has been watching my children suffer from their brother's murder."

For several years after Christopher's death Mika felt trapped in a horrible cycle she could not get out of. One moment she tried to be grateful for what she had left in life, but soon she would be overpowered with anger because of what she was now missing. Even everyday situations would affect her in a negative way.

"I would be angry when I heard people laugh. I thought, *How dare you laugh?* Today, I have allowed myself to laugh again, but I will never feel half as happy as I did before Christopher's death. Happiness will never again come from the gut. Because a part of my flesh and blood died that day with Christopher. And I have spent almost twenty-five years walking around with a mask on. I have been too afraid to confront my deepest feelings. But now I face my demons and deal with my emotions. It is painful and difficult moving forward," Mika acknowledges.

However, one thing that has brought her some measure of joy is teaching other children about personal safety. Mika accomplishes this through an organisation called Christopher's Clubhouse, which she founded a few years after her son's death. She has taught hundreds of children through the years, and there is one message she has conveyed to all of them:

"I tell them that people are like the weather. Most of the time it is sunny and nice, but you never know when you will meet a thunderstorm. Therefore it is important to be prepared when you do," Mika says.

To prepare the children for the unexpected she puts them through realistic situations, and she provides them with answers regarding how to respond if they are approached by a stranger.

"We raise our children telling them not to kick and hit, so they need to practise how to actually fight back when a bad person tries to grab and harm them. And, not least, we need to teach them that it is okay to do it," Mika notes.

She says that only Timothy Buss knows for sure what happened when Christopher was taken, but Mika believes her son was first approached by the killer at the riverside and then again when Christopher rode his bike home.

"And if Christopher had just known that a child should never approach a car with a stranger he might still be alive. I cannot change the past, but I can have an impact on the future by causing awareness of this problem that too many children become victims of, but that too few Americans are aware of," Mika explains.

She says that in today's world the biggest threat to children is often online predators. Children are going online when they are as young as toddler age, and they are learning how to navigate the vast virtual world; and as they glean that knowledge, the world becomes smaller to them. Today, both children and teens are able to communicate with anonymous and unknown *others*, feeling safe behind the glass of their computer or phone screen. But predators are lurking in our living rooms, according to Mika.

"They are in our homes by virtue of the online world and the kids that communicate with them. The slow manipulation and grooming of a predator takes place without a child even realising it. The online predators are patient, lying in wait for weeks and months until the opportunity arises to 'pounce'," Mika says.

She observes that the conversations are innocent and benign at first, with the predator gaining the trust of the prey, until the vulnerable child becomes willing to provide the predator with personal information—or, worse, to meet the predator in person.

"It is imperative that parents become allies with their child in the world of cyber-reality. Parents should let the child know they can always let the adults in the house know if someone they have never met tries to communicate with them. Open, honest communication is [at] the forefront to allowing our kids to be online," she says.

Mika observes that kids are afraid their privileges will be taken away if they receive a solicitation, inappropriate photograph, or bullying text. Therefore, parents need to assure their kids that as long as the child is following the rules, they will not lose their right to be online.

Mika believes there are also other ways to keep children safe from the harm of sexual predators.

Four months after Christopher's death, a sex offender registry law was enacted in Illinois. Christopher's death was one of the principal crimes that lead to the law. However, Mika wishes the registry had been in place earlier, and that another child didn't have to die at the hands of an unknown sexual predator.

To keep children safe Mika has since stressed the importance of laws that protect children and keep dangerous criminals behind bars. She has advocated for financial appropriations that will give law enforcement officials increased funding they can use to pursue the predators.

"I have worked with state and federal legislators to increase the strength of our laws… especially those [that] relate to sex offender registries. Knowing where the predators live and work is important to protect our children. However, even more important is teaching our children how to be safe and protect themselves," Mika says.

To get out her message about child safety she has repeatedly worked with the media, even though she has not always had a productive relationship with reporters. When Timothy Buss was on trial Mika would have to run through a doorway beneath the court building in order to avoid the media, which was constantly pursuing her in order to get a photograph. A member of the media once even brought her news that was devastating to her. Timothy Buss had been sentenced to death, but one day the *Washington Post* called Mika and asked how she felt about the state of Illinois deciding to commute all death sentences in the state to life imprisonment.

"Authorities never bothered to call and tell [me]. And in general too many parents are told through the media that their children have been found dead. When a parent finds out this way it is as if their child is just another statistic. However, if a police officer sits down and tells [you] it becomes personal, and your child is remembered as a human being. Your child was a person and not just a quote in a news piece," Mika observes.

Mika is also hurt when friends do not understand the pain that parents go through. She specifically recalls an episode a few years back, when she was asked to be a spokesperson for an event organised by the National Center for Missing and Exploited Children in Los Angeles. The event had been highly publicised and would be broadcast on television, as the organisation wanted to draw attention to children who were missing in Los Angeles. Mika had been asked to be the face of the organisation throughout the day. When she told this to a close friend who was a struggling actress, the friend just bursted out that Mika was so lucky that she got to be on television all day.

"I was so hurt by that statement. I would want to be [any] other [place] than on television because I was there for all the wrong reasons," Mika recalls.

And she was also sitting in the courtroom for all the wrong reasons when the trial against Timothy Buss started. However, during the trial she would learn another important thing about her son. A young boy testified that while Christopher was at the boat launch the kid had suggested that they ride their bikes into the river. But Christopher had refused to do so. He needed to leave the boat launch, because he had to get back home to his mom on time.

10

DOMESTIC VIOLENCE

As you spend the next sixty seconds reading these lines, twenty people in America will become victims of domestic violence. According to the National Coalition Against Domestic Violence, this equates to more than 10 million victims over the course of a single year.

Overall, one in four women, and one in seven men, will have severe physical violence inflicted on them by an intimate partner at some point during their lifetime. (The term *severe physical violence* includes beating, burning, or strangling by an intimate partner.) Violence perpetrated on a victim by an intimate partner accounts for 15 percent of all violent crime. In the most extreme cases, the violence leads to the innocent partner becoming a homicide victim. In the other cases the domestic violence can escalate to abduction, where a partner is held hostage against his or her will.

For fifteen years Marianne Asher-Chapman has been search-ing for her daughter, **Angela**, after she became the victim of her husband's brutality.

A FORCEFUL MOTHER

Missing: Michelle Angela Yarnell

Date of Birth: 05/20/1975

Missing From: Ivy Bend, Missouri

Missing Since: 10/25/2003 (28 years old)

Classification: Endangered Missing

Interview: Marianne Asher-Chapman, mother of Angela

It was a cold February morning when Marianne walked through the nature area that she helped plant in a field close to her house. The Missouri winter had been harsh but by no means as tough on her as the four months leading up to it.

Every day the forty-nine-year-old woman prayed that she would soon have some degree of certainty regarding her daughter's whereabouts. Not knowing whether her daughter Angie were dead after she had disappeared without a trace over fall was proving too difficult for Marianne.

She wasn't a strong believer, but as she walked through the field she couldn't help but to pray out loud: "God, please give me a sign!"

Her prayer was answered. Immediately, a doe appeared from nowhere. The animal was bigger and more beautiful than any she had seen before. And as it peacefully stood in front of her, the magnificent beast looked directly into Marianne's eyes.

"I just got down on my knees and said: 'Thank you, God'. I asked Him for a sign and He gave me one. That moment I knew that Angie was there with him in Heaven," Marianne says.

When the doe disappeared Marianne finally accepted that her daughter had been the victim of a vicious crime that had led to her death. Marianne just did not know how and where to find her remains.

The mother's uncertainty about her daughter's whereabouts began on the afternoon of October 25, 2003. The entire family had been invited for dinner at Marianne's house in Holts Summit, Missouri, but her twenty-eight-year-old daughter never showed up. Instead, her husband did.

Michael Yarnell was a quiet man. His mother-in-law would later describe him as an introvert who would hardly put two words together in the company of others. But that afternoon he spoke like never before. Michael Yarnell was heartbroken. He told Marianne that his wife of three years, Angie, had left him for another man.

The family felt for Michael and comforted him even though Marianne found it hard to believe that her daughter would do such a thing. She had always been a devoted wife, and although she might have left her husband by filing for a divorce she would never leave her mother by running away with another man.

"I was terribly sick with throat cancer," Marianne explains. "Angie supported me all the way through, and there was no way she was gonna leave without saying goodbye."

The next morning, Marianne decided to pay the police department in Morgan County a visit, as there was still no sign of her daughter. The encounter with officers disillusioned Marianne even further.

Angie had never been in trouble with the law. She did not do drugs, she did not live an obscene life, and she never caused problems for anyone.

"But she lived in Ivy Bend, Morgan County—a community known for housing criminals and drug addicts," Marianne notes. "Therefore the police department right away labeled her as such, and they would not take her disappearance seriously. At first they refused to file a missing persons report, saying that she probably did run off with that other man. So I had to stand my ground and force the report through. The police department should have been more than willing to help me," Marianne says.

The disbelief on law enforcement's part and their unwillingness to try to find Angie paralysed Marianne. She could not find a single soul who could help her locate Angie or tell her what to do, although she searched desperately for someone to come to her aid. The disappointment she felt towards the police department, along with her determination to fight for justice *and* beat her cancer, grew within her.

"I constantly cried while struggling to get through everyday life and surviving my illness. There was a time where I could not even speak, but I knew that I needed my voice back. Because my voice was the voice of Angie. And I needed to speak out to put focus on Angie's case and to get justice for her," Marianne explains.

Before her daughter's disappearance Marianne knew little of how the justice system worked, and when she learned how the system actually functioned she was shocked. According to Marianne, the police always profile a missing person to decide whether they want to investigate a disappearance. Citizens with noteworthy backgrounds are a priority, while anyone who has a social problem like poverty, drug abuse, and unemployment are left to themselves, with no help.

Marianne says she has reviewed hundreds of cases of missing persons since her daughter's disappearance—cases where the police failed in their obligation to protect and serve their citizens. Leads were not investigated and evidence was ignored or even destroyed.

But Marianne grew determined. She was not going to leave her daughter's destiny in the hands of the local police department. If the investigators would not give Angie the attention Marianne felt she deserved then her mother would get it for her.

"I became very forceful and realised that if you want something you have to go and take it," Marianne explains. And she wanted her daughter back. So she put up billboards offering a $5,000 reward for any information leading to her daughter's whereabouts.

"Those billboards were so big you could not help but notice them. Unfortunately they did not help me [in] finding Angie."

Besides putting up billboards Marianne handed out thousands of flyers. After she had made sure everyone in the local community had received one she drove to other states looking for her daughter. She never rested in her search for Angie…and soon the police department wouldn't either.

Marianne constantly phoned investigators, asking if there had been any progress in the case. The officers were often rude to her. And still the police department did not do much to find Angie, the mother observes.

THE BILLBOARDS

When a postcard from a small town in Harrison, Arkansas, arrived in Marianne's mailbox ten days after her daughter's disappearance, it almost seemed as if Marianne had been wasting investigators' time. The postcard that is in the police files today says:

Mom, we are going to Texas tomorrow to visit Gary's family. Will write you when we are settled. Love Angie

The postcard made Marianne wonder if her daughter had left her husband for another man after all.

"We all felt sorry for Michael, and a month after Angie's disappearance we had him over for Thanksgiving. I remember how he sat at the table just crying. The same thing happened when he was here for Christmas," Marianne recalls about the first holidays after her daughter had gone missing.

The holiday season was a turning point for Marianne. Angie knew how important this time of year was for her mother, and if Angie were still alive she would certainly have come home, even if she had fallen in love with a new man. When she failed to show up, Marianne no longer had any doubts. Foul play had been involved in her daughter's disappearance.

Marianne acted on her suspicion—and so did a reporter from a local newspaper. The reporter noticed the big billboards and how Marianne seemed to be alone in her search for Angie. Together, they looked for a perpetrator. One step they took was to have a handwriting expert examine the postcard that Marianne had received shortly after Angie's disappearance.

Marianne always doubted that her daughter was the author of the postcard, because the handwriting appeared to differ from Angie's. When the handwriting expert examined the card she concluded that the handwriting did not belong to Angie. She also compared the postcard to a handwritten statement that Angie's husband had given to the police when his wife was reported missing. The handwriting expert's conclusion was shocking. Michael Yarnell had written the postcard. There was no doubt. He had been lying when he claimed the author was his "deceitful wife", Angie.

"I was not surprised," Marianne says. "All the time I had suspected that he knew more than he was telling. I knew he had killed Angie."

With increased media focus Marianne once again confronted the police department, asking for action. She brought the postcard to their attention—although it was not the first time she had done so.

Marianne says she handed the postcard over to an investigator right after she had received it, asking him to examine it for DNA evidence. The postcard's sender would have left traces of spit when he or she licked the stamp and attached it to the card.

"The investigator promised to send the postcard to a lab for testing, but when he retired years later they found the postcard was still in his drawer. Had he just done his job, and as [he had] promised, we would have known much earlier who was responsible for Angie's disappearance," Marianne says.

Four years after Angie went missing Michael Yarnell was named a person of interest in the investigation—among other reasons because of the graphologist's findings. But before the police could question him, Michael Yarnell took off.

Once again Marianne went to the police department, this time because she figured the best way to find Michael would be by filing a missing person's report in his name. Marianne was right. Soon after filing the missing person's report, Marianne's gambit paid off.

Michael Yarnell had applied for a job at an air force base in Biloxi, Mississippi. The air force ran a background check on him, and Mr. Yarnell showed up as a missing person. He was immediately transferred to Missouri.

When confronted with the analysis of the handwriting expert, Michael Yarnell admitted he had written the postcard, but he claimed he did it out of a good heart and that he just wanted to give Marianne peace of mind so she would not worry about Angie being dead. The postcard was meant to serve as proof that Angie was still alive. Later, however, Michael Yarnell confessed to killing Angie by accident.

According to Michael Yarnell, the couple got into an argument the day Marianne had invited them over for dinner, and he pushed Angie off their deck at the house. Unfortunately she fell and hit a rock.

She died shortly thereafter. Michael explained that he panicked and drove off with his wife's body in the car before dumping her body in the Lake of the Ozarks. When investigators searched the lake they did not find any evidence confirming his story. The prosecutor tried to charge Michael Yarnell with murder, but eventually offered him a deal in which the killer would plead guilty to involuntary manslaughter. In 2009, Michael Yarnell was sentenced to seven years in prison—but he served only four years of his term.

"In my mind he got away with murder. The police could not find the body, and he would not tell them where it was, so without this important evidence the prosecution was afraid to lose in court and therefore offered him a plea bargain. In my opinion he should have had a sentence that fits his crime. Four years for murder is nothing," Marianne says.

MISSOURI MISSING

Her former son-in-law's confession never came as a surprise to Marianne. When Michael Yarnell said that Angie left with another man he had also said that she had not taken any of her belongings with her. Her purse, her clothes, and all of her other personal belongings were still in the house. The only thing Angie had apparently taken with her was a collage of pictures that had been hanging on a wall.

"The minute he told me Angie had taken the collage, I knew[…] where she had been murdered. She must have had massive head trauma, and therefore had splattered blood all over the pictures. I am sure he removed the pictures to erase evidence," Marianne speculates.

Today, Marianne regrets that she did not accuse Michael Yarnell of murder earlier. She kept quiet, she says, because if she had accused him publicly she would also have made the crime real, a fact of life for her.

"I did not want it to be. I wanted Angie to be alive and to come home. You cannot help wishful thinking," Marianne explains.

Even though it has been more than fifteen years since Angie's disappearance, Marianne at times still imagines her daughter walking through the front door. And that imagery will probably accompany Marianne until the day she has tangible proof of where her daughter's remains are.

"This man was so successful in hiding her body, and he will not tell where she is though he has admitted to having killed her. It does not add up. But one thing is sure. Not knowing where her remains are is the worse," Marianne says.

After Michael Yarnell was incarcerated she sent him money for months, trying to show him some tenderness. Not because she forgave him for what he had done, but because she wanted him to work with her.

She also visited him in prison, to ask where she could find her daughter. But while talking about the visit Marianne quickly corrects herself.

"No, I did not ask. I *begged* him to tell, but he would not. He finds control over me by not being willing to tell where Angie is," Marianne says.

Marianne will never give up on trying to find her daughter. She always keeps a shovel in her car, so she can dig for her daughter in case a sudden notion of Angie's presence comes to her. To Marianne the worst time of year is winter, when it's impossible to dig because the ground is frozen. On the other hand she appreciates when deer season begins. Throughout the years, remains of missing people have often been discovered by hunters who have stumbled over their bones. Marianne always writes to different hunting associations when the season starts, both to remind and inform them of all the missing persons reported in Missouri.

"Too many are missing," she says.

And Marianne would know. She was so disappointed with the local police department and the plea bargain Michael Yarnell was offered that she is now deeply involved in a nonprofit organisation called Missouri Missing.

Marianne cofounded the organisation in 2007, after she heard of another mother looking in vain for a daughter.

Peggy Florence's daughter, Jasmine Haslag, was last seen when she left her house to pick up her children. She never arrived at their father's house; instead, her car was found hidden out of sight in a field on a nearby highway. The car's licence plate and battery had been removed from the vehicle. Today, the thirty-year-old woman is still missing.

Marianne offered her help to Peggy Florence. Later, the two women founded Missouri Missing, whose mission is to:

Provide a voice for the missing and unidentified who can no longer speak for themselves. Provide support for families who have missing loved ones through an outreach program. Educate and provide public awareness of the impact of missing persons in Missouri. Work closely with law enforcement and provide as much assistance as possible to individuals and law enforcement agencies in the prevention, investigation and prosecution of all cases involving missing persons in Missouri...

(Source: *www.missourimissing.org*)

Marianne says she tries to offer others the help she never had and to make sure that the relatives of the approximately 900 individuals who are currently missing in Missouri (according to the organisation) maintain hope that they will eventually find their loved ones, just as Marianne has never given up on finding Angie.

She has not lost hope that one day Michael Yarnell will come around and tell her where she is.

"He cannot be charged with the crime again because of a double jeopardy law, so he has nothing to lose, there is no reason for him not to tell. He can only become a better person by confessing to what really happened to Angie. I hope he will realise this," Marianne explains.

For that reason she is glad that she never succeeded in doing what she contemplated for a moment while she was visiting Wal-Mart one day shortly after Michael Yarnell had been released from prison. She was in the store searching for vitamins.

"I was looking down in the cart, and when I looked up Michael Yarnell was right in front of me, just five feet away. I did not know how to handle the situation, so I panicked," Marianne says.

What happened next shook Marianne to the core.

A KILLER'S HUG

Marianne was paralysed by the sight of her daughter's killer. Michael Yarnell put his arms out as though he was going to hug her. But before he could embrace her, Marianne regained her forceful attitude, and her self-assurance.

"I said directly to his face that next month it would be ten years since I had lost Angie and I asked him again if he would tell [me] where she was. He just replied 'I already told you how she died,'" Marianne says.

The next minute she ran out of the supermarket and jumped in to her car. Today, she is not proud of her reaction, because for the minutes that followed she almost became a killer herself.

"I sat in my car for fifteen to twenty minutes just waiting for him to come out of the store. I wanted to run him over. I am glad he didn't come out before I realised how easy it is for a person to snap. But I did not want to be as bad a person as he is, so finally I just went home. Today I am not proud of the fact that I wanted to run him down," Marianne confides.

However, she does have one regret. When she met Michael Yarnell in the supermarket he was with a very beautiful woman. Today, she regrets that she did not look up the woman to tell her what her new man was capable of.

"I believe Angie is not the first woman he has harmed, and I am afraid she is not the last," Marianne speculates.

Several times she has thought about filing a civil lawsuit against Michael Yarnell, as this might force him to tell what he did to Angie's corpse, Marianne says.

"All I am asking for is her remains, and I won't rest till I have tangible proof of her death," the mother says.

But after Michael Yarnell was convicted, finding Angie's remains did not become any easier. After the convicted killer was put behind bars, the police decided to close the case.

Once again, Marianne proved to be a fighter who would not accept authorities not helping those in need.

"I went up to the sheriff's department and explained that I was going to file another missing case report for Angie. They said I could not do that twice, but I kept asking if they could then tell me where Angie's body is. If they couldn't I would insist on filing another report. So they agreed to close the criminal part but reopen the missing part," Marianne says.

She is proud to have shown the strength to force the authorities to reopen the case, but Marianne remains sad that her actions released the police department off the media hook, as she calls it. Every time the media want to hold the police department accountable for their work and their search for Angie, the department always excuses itself by saying they cannot comment on an open investigation, Marianne says. However, this does not mean that Marianne will let the department off of *her* hook.

"I have never been able to come up with a good answer for why it is important for me to have Angie's remains. I have been told by other parents that it is hard going to your child's grave, but I think that at least it is not as hard as not having a grave to go to. I would like to have the option," Marianne explains.

Although both Marianne and the media are not getting the answers they would like from the police department, the work of the local authorities does not go unnoticed.

In 2017, the Hollywood movie *Three Billboards Outside Ebbing, Missouri* was released in the United States. The movie takes place in the town of Ebbing, where a mother, Mildred Hayes, is grieving over the murder of her teenage daughter, Angela. Mildred is angry with the police department because of the lack of progress in the investigation into Angela's death. Venting her frustration, Mildred rents three abandoned billboards near her home then posts the following messages on them:

RAPED WHILE DYING
AND STILL NO ARRESTS?
HOW COME, CHIEF WILLOUGHBY?

Frances McDormand plays Mildred, a role for which she won an Academy award for best actress. It is said that Mildred's character is based on Marianne, who afterwards was often described as "the real-life billboard mother". When Marianne went to see the movie she recognised herself in it.

"Quite a bit of the movie reminds [me] about my life and Angie's case. They even named the victim, Angela, after my daughter," Marianne observes.

Watching the movie in the cinema with her friends gave her goose bumps. Particularly because one of the scenes reflects one of the most crucial turning points in Marianne's life.

At one point in the movie, Mildred plants flowers under one of the billboards. When she looks up a deer appears—just as when Marianne was walking through her nature park, asking God for a sign.

"When I watched that scene I could feel that Angie was right there in the cinema with me," Marianne says.

She is happy with the movie, as she believes it helps to focus the public's attention onto Angie's case. The more publicity the better, Marianne says, as she hopes the attention will someday allow someone to step forward with the information she needs to find Angie, and her peace of mind. Until that day Marianne tries to keep in touch with her daughter by writing letters to her loved one, as do many moms of the missing.

TIME AFTER TIME

When she walked around outside her house four months after her daughter's disappearance, she carried a notebook containing letters she had written to her daughter. Today, she has more than twenty-five such notebooks.

"When I walked through that field accepting she was dead I could not believe she had already been gone for four months. Now it has been almost 200 months. Just like people convicted of crimes, we the victims also count time. We also feel [as if we are] in prison," Marianne says. She explains how she started the first letter: "This is day no. 42 since I have heard from you", she wrote.

Today, she writes just to relieve her head, and she writes in only very artistic notebooks, as Angie was a lover of art. At times when she writes she refers to songs that Angie liked. Especially Cindy Lauper's song "Time After Time". Marianne starts to recite the lyrics:

If you're lost you can look and you will find me
Time after time…
If you fall I will catch you, I will be waiting
Time after time …
(Excerpted from "Time After Time", by Cindy Lauper)

Marianne feels the lyrics describe her and Angie's relationship to each other even today, when they do not have one another's company to enjoy in the physical world. Marianne starts to laugh when she describes how crazy Angie was about Cyndi Lauper.

"We had to shave one side of her head and dye her hair so she could look just like her," Marianne recalls.

Today, Marianne doesn't write letters as often as she used to. Perhaps this is because she doesn't need to. Instead, she spends a lot of time helping other parents who have lost their children. She also visits prisons, to teach inmates and tell them how their crimes affect the victims.

"I see life as: Maybe all this had to happen. Perhaps I had to go through this pain, and perhaps Angie had to die, because it has given me the chance of teaching and speaking about domestic violence. Perhaps that saves others [from] becoming victims. Maybe that is how my life was meant to be. I survived throat cancer because Angie and others need my voice. I feel it is my duty to help those in need of it, and it is my honour if I can help just one person [move on] to a better life or [save a] life if just one of these offenders I speak to stop[s] being violent towards his family. If so I know Angie would be extremely proud of me," Marianne says.

For more than twenty years Marianne herself was a victim of domestic violence. Therefore, she finds it especially sad that she was not by Angie's side, in a position to help her own daughter, when she needed it.

"I survived twenty years of domestic violence in my previous marriage. Angie did not even survive three years. I feel guilty for not having seen her being violated. She never told me, but after she went missing her neighbours told me that she often had black eyes and was abused. I cannot forgive myself for not having been there to help her.

But I can find her and bring her home, and I know that one day I will. I will never, never, never give up," Marianne vows.

11
THE IMPACT OF DNA

Jared Scheierl was walking home from a cafe in Cold Spring, Minnesota, when a car pulled over. The driver asked Jared for directions, but his actual intentions were to force the twelve-year-old boy into the car. After sexually assaulting the boy, the man used a cloth to wipe down Jared's snowsuit. Before taking him back into town he told the boy to roll around in the snow so all physical evidence would be removed from his clothes.

The assault of Jared Scheierl took place in January 1989. Only nine months earlier another boy had been kidnapped and assaulted in the nearby town of St. Joseph.

Jacob Wetterling was eleven years old and on his way home from a store when he was taken. Jacob never returned home. Thirty years later his parents finally found out what had happened to their son.

During all that time, police suspected that Jacob Wetterling had been taken and killed by the same man who assaulted Jared Scheierl, but they had no lead in either of the two cases until 2015. The Minnesota Bureau of Criminal Apprehension (BCA) had previously tested a sample from Scheierl's clothing—and suddenly they had a DNA match. The perpetrator's name was Danny Heinrich, but the statute of limitations had expired, so he could not be charged with the crime. However, a search warrant was granted. When detectives searched Danny Heinrich's house they found child pornography. The subsequent pornography charges led to Heinrich admitting in court that he had assaulted Jared Scheierl and killed Jacob Wetterling.

Advances in DNA testing over the many years since the assault on Jacob Scheierl had motivated BCA to complete a new round of testing of the evidence found on Scheierl's clothes. Matching DNA samples from hair, semen, saliva, and blood to a suspected perpetrator's DNA was by then much easier. When the crime had taken place forensic scientists were able to conclude only that DNA from "two or more people" was present on Scheierl's clothes; that is, a mixture of DNA was present. Now, almost thirty years on, advances in forensics allowed scientists to identify a person from a single strand of DNA.

In Jared Scheierl's case the police were able to use the original hair samples Heinrich had given them immediately after the crime. By using the more modern methods available to them in 2015, detectives were able to prove that Danny Heinrich was the perpetrator in the assaults of both Jared Scheierl and Jacob Wetterling. Prosecutors then offered Heinrich the plea deal, and he served twenty years in prison on child pornography charges. He also admitted to the crimes against the two boys and lead investigators to Jacob Wetterling's remains.

The cases involving the boys from Minnesota are just two of the thousands of cases in which DNA samples have led law enforcement officers to the perpetrators of heinous crimes, such as the abduction and killing of Jacob Wetterling. Often, the criminals are found because law enforcement agencies have previously registered the DNA of the convicted felon in their DNA databases. The number of samples in

DNA databases is constantly growing. The National DNA Index (NDIS) contains over 13,823,140 offender profiles, 3,568,200 arrestee profiles, and 944,750 forensic profiles as of May 2019. But according to Joan Berry the databases still have a long way to go. In 2004, her daughter, **Johnia,** was murdered.

Although DNA evidence was recovered from the crime scene, no match was made to any DNA samples in any database, in spite of the fact that law enforcement expected the perpetrator to be the kind of person who had been in and out of prison. Since that time, Joan Berry has tried to convince legislators to register more convicted felons in DNA databases all across America. According to Joan, the more robust a database is the more likely it is to not only help identify and catch the killers, but to lead investigators to the individuals who have been abducted, making it easier for investigators to find the victims and save them before they are murdered, as Jacob Wetterling was after he was kidnapped.

A DATABASE OF HOPE
Victim: Johnia Berry
Date of Birth: 08/26/1983
Scene of Crime: Knoxville, Tennessee
Crime Committed: 12/06/2004 (21 years old)
Classification: Murder
Interview: Joan Berry, mother of Johnia

Johnia Berry was spending that December night shopping for toys. When she returned to her apartment she began sorting and wrapping the toys for the children with whom she worked at a learning centre. Every year leading up to Christmas Johnia volunteered for various charitable services for children in need, and that evening she went to bed happy. But she did not know what fate had in store for her a few hours later.

Sometime during the early morning hours of the next day, a thief broke into Johnia's apartment, searching for car keys in the living room. When he did not find what he was looking for he went into the bedroom where Johnia was peacefully sleeping. Johnia was awakened by the thief. She was frightened, and she repeatedly asked, "Who are you, what are you doing here?" The thief told her to chill out, but Johnia began screaming and tried to escape.

The thief stabbed Johnia more than twenty times before leaving the apartment empty-handed, but with murder on his conscience.

Johnia fought for her life. In spite of the numerous stab wounds she still managed to stumble down two flights of stairs then knock on her neighbour's doors, desperately seeking the same charitable help she had always so gladly offered others. But no one was there for Johnia. After several minutes she collapsed and died at the age of twenty-one years.

"Johnia was a beautiful, ambitious, hard-working girl who was one of the youngest females to be accepted into Thomas Cooley Law School in Michigan," her mother Joan proudly says. "After some consideration she decided to do something else. She was very caring and wanted to help others, especially children. Prior to being killed she returned to Tennessee and worked at Peninsula Hospital with adolescents."

Johnia's mother received a call at five a.m., after the brutal assault on her daughter. Just like her daughter, she collapsed to the floor. She was overcome by the shock of what she had heard.

The call had come from UT Hospital in Knoxville, informing Joan that a young woman had been brought into the hospital without identification. Health care workers at the facility had suspected the woman was Johnia Berry, and they needed someone to come in and identify the body.

For four hours Joan and Johnia's father drove from their home in Atlanta, Georgia, to the hospital in Tennessee. They alerted their two sons as to what had happened and told them to get to the hospital as fast as possible.

"Driving there for so many hours and not knowing if my daughter had died was just horrible," Joan recalls.

On arrival Joan was met by her two sons. Kelly opened his arms to hug his mother and give her the devastating news: "It is Johnia, mom."

Joan says no words can express the pain she felt when she realised her daughter had been killed.

"Since that day there has been a hole in my heart and mind that can never be filled. Today, almost fifteen years later, I still think about Johnia every day, and I still break down and cry when I do. I miss her, and I know I will until the day I die. Time does not heal all wounds," Joan says.

At first Joan could not believe that her daughter had been killed. She always provided a safe upbringing for all three of her children—she was proud of each of them. Her daughter was independent and striving to start an exciting new phase of her life: Johnia had just moved to Knoxville six weeks prior to her murder.

In fact, Johnia had just finished her final classes at East Tennessee State University (ETSU). Her plan was to become a graduate student in psychology at the University of Tennessee in Knoxville. She seemed to have a bright future ahead of her...until the intruder proved that the most vicious crimes can happen to anyone, anywhere.

"My advice is never take life for granted, and let people you love know. They might not be here tomorrow. Because now I know every-one can become [a victim] of evil," Joan says. She adds that ten days after her daughter was buried, she and Johnia's father walked across the stage at ETSU in Johnson City, Tennessee, to accept Johnia's diploma.

After the brutal murder Joan had to make a lot of decisions. The first thing she had to do was to find out who murdered her only daughter and answer the question: *How are we going to go on without her?* Only some time later did the reality of her daughter's death sink in. It was "a long and heartbreaking process," Joan says.

While dealing with the heartbreaking emotions she was content to know one thing: It was probably just a question of time before law enforcement would identify, locate, and arrest her daughter's killer.

When the killer stabbed Johnia, her roommate, Jason Aymami, woke up to Johnia's screaming. He immediately ran out of his room and hurried into the hallway, where he met Johnia's killer. The intruder punched Jason then stabbed him in his chest and face. In spite of being attacked, Jason Aymami managed to run off to a nearby gas station, where he asked the clerk to call 911. The roommate provided a detailed description of the perpetrator, so a police sketch of his image could be created.

When investigators arrived at the crime scene they collected three different blood samples: Johnia's, Jason's, and the killer's.

"The evidence was right there," Joan notes. "We had the killer's DNA, so I was very optimistic about the police finding the perpetrator. It was not until later that I found out that the national database lacked critical information to help solve the crime," she explains.

Both Joan and investigators expected the perpetrator to be the kind of person who had been in and out of prison, but they could not get a match, because his DNA had never been registered by law enforcement. The evidence found at the crime scene was so solid that police began collecting DNA samples from inmates around the country to try and find a match. Over time the police would complete more than four hundred DNA tests, but still no match showed up. Joan's optimism turned to frustration.

"I just knew in my heart and mind that Johnia's killer committed crimes prior to her murder, so it was terrible finding out that there was no database with his DNA. We were so close to knowing who he was, and yet so far," Joan says.

Three years passed before Joan found out who killed her daughter.

Taylor Olson was just twenty-two years old and an active repeat offender in 2004, when the murder was committed. He committed several crimes during the period 2004 to 2007. Although charged several times for credit card theft, forgery, driving without a driver's licence, harassment, aggravated burglary, and theft, it wasn't until July 2007, when he was charged for violating his probation order, that he voluntarily submitted a sample of his DNA. Shortly thereafter, the District Attorney General's Office in Knox County concluded that Taylor Olson was Johnia's killer. The DNA evidence left no doubt. He was now charged with first-degree murder. Just as Joan had predicted, the killer was guilty of several violations. The lead investigator in the case called Joan and informed her of the arrest. The call came on the anniversary of Joan and Michael's wedding.

"I think this was Johnia's gift to us," Joan says.

Her parents had always celebrated their anniversary with Johnia, but this year they went to her grave, where they sat and talked to Johnia while planting roses and celebrating that her suspected killer was locked up.

Taylor Olson lived with a friend, Noah Cox, down the road from Johnia's apartment. According to the *Knoxville News Sentinel,* when Taylor Olson was arrested he told detectives that Johnia's death had been an accident.

He and Noah Cox had been drinking beers and smoking marijuana all night while also breaking into cars. Later they split up, and Taylor Olson went looking for an open apartment door so he could steal car keys. But when he went into Johnia's apartment he woke someone up, and a fight broke out:

"It was so dark," Taylor Olson told investigators in a September 23, 2007 interview. *"I was looking for some keys and then, someone said, 'Who are you' or 'What are you doing' or something…then I heard like a yell and I just felt a pain. I just freaked out.…I didn't see a face or anything.…I got [the knife] away, and it didn't seem like I stabbed anybody, it seemed like a fight or something, and then I just ran."*

(Source: Knoxville News Sentinel)

When the investigators asked Taylor Olson if he had broken into the apartment with anyone he replied: "No one was with me."

After the arrest the district attorney began preparing for the upcoming trial. Joan had been preparing for it for three years; she even kept a journal with questions she was going to ask her daughter's suspected killer. Although she wanted answers, she was dreading the moment she had to confront the cold-blooded murderer in court.

"Happiness over the arrest quickly turned to fear. I started worrying about if they had evidence enough to convict him. And I could not stop thinking about how I would react when I faced the man who killed my daughter," Joan says.

But she never had to. When officers checked on Taylor Olson shortly after midnight he had hanged himself with a sheet tied to a clothes' hook in his cell.

"He had killed my daughter in a cowardly way and now he chose a coward's way out. I was so angry because he would never be held accountable for his crimes. Today I see it differently. I constantly asked God how I was gonna get through court. When Taylor Olson committed suicide God answered me. In my heart I believe my family was blessed when he killed himself. For many reasons," Joan says.

Since her daughter's death Joan has been part of a support group for relatives of murder victims. Often, their pain continues after the perpetrator has been convicted, because in many cases a new round of court hearings starts when the prisoner gets the chance to apply for parole.

One of the victims Joan met is a woman who was abducted as a teenager, along with her friend. A man forced the girls into the woods, where he molested and killed the woman's friend before the woman herself managed to escape. Almost thirty years later she is confronted by her abductor (and her friend's killer) every time she has to testify at parole hearings, where she explains why she believes the convicted murderer should remain in prison for the gruesome crimes he committed.

"Victims' wounds are ripped open every time they have to fight to keep the killers in prison," Joan says. "Taylor Olson's suicide means we do not have to go through that nightmare again and again every year till the day we die."

When Taylor Olson committed suicide half a year after his arrest, he left letters for his family. The letters upset Joan because when Taylor Olson took his own life, he left instructions regarding his funeral and what songs he would like his family to play in church.

"Johnia never had the chance of writing any letters saying goodbye to her family before she was killed, and she never had any chance of telling her family how she would like her funeral," Joan says.

Another reason Joan is annoyed is that Taylor Olson accused another man of killing Johnia and claimed that he was innocent in his letters. Prosecutors, however, never charged Noah Cox, the man Taylor Olson named as the killer.

When he committed suicide law enforcement reviewed the evidence one more time and concluded that Taylor Olson was the killer. They had fingerprints that matched the one found on a knife in Johnia's apartment, and his DNA was a perfect match of the DNA from one of the blood samples taken from the crime scene.

"Why would he commit suicide if he did not commit the crime?" Joan asks.

She continues:

"There is no doubt he killed her. His DNA was solid proof. And because DNA is such a significant [piece of] evidence in murder cases, it is so important that we register criminals' DNA all across America, so that we can solve crimes and prevent criminals from committing any further offenses—and, most importantly, a DNA database can save lives. Imagine how useful it can be if a person is abducted and the kidnapper leaves DNA at the crime scene. A database can lead directly to the perpetrator and bring back home the abducted," Joan says. She then mentions how important saving other parents' children from abductors and killers is to her, because she knows how painful it is to lose a child.

Because of her belief in the power DNA holds to help investigators solve crimes, Joan decided to post a message on the internet shortly after Taylor Olson killed himself.

In the very early morning hours on December 6, 2004, Taylor Lee Olson entered my daughter's apartment. He was looking to steal. When he didn't find what he wanted he went into Johnia's bedroom where she was sleeping, and there he took her life. He didn't even know my daughter, but he stole her life! Police called it OVER KILL! There was DNA left in Johnia's apartment, but no match for it in the database. Three long years we waited for answers, praying for justice! There are no words to express the pain my family and I have endured. Each day is a struggle, I miss Johnia so very much! I will be sad until the day I die!

You never know if a tragedy like this could happen to a member of your family. I must say, I never did. Especially, not at 4 AM. When your child is sleeping, you think she is SAFE! I ask you to please think about this. And ask yourself, shouldn't we as parents do everything in our power to protect our loved ones? Please encourage your State Legislators to do their job – DNA Laws are needed!

Joan was busy not only creating a website in memory of her daughter—where she posted the words about the power DNA holds as an investigative tool—she was also busy contacting legislators in order to try to change the current law.

"We are always told by legislators that it is all about 'the dollar', as it is expensive, creating these databases. But how do you put a price tag on my daughter's life?" Joan asks. She answers the question herself, saying that she cannot imagine a better way to spend taxpayers' money than to create a safer society.

Joan explains: "Our system does not work as it should. We should have databases all over America."

Joan started to lobby for the creation of a database in Tennessee, where DNA is registered even when a perpetrator commits a minor crime. She met with legislators numerous times. And after two years her efforts finally paid off. On May 9, 2007 the Johnia Berry Act was passed.

Lawmakers in Nashville unanimously passed the act, which states that anyone arrested for a violent felony is required to give a DNA sample and that the sample must be registered in a statewide database. Today, thirty states have passed laws making it possible to register some form of DNA for felony arrests.

"DNA is the fingerprinting of our time, so all fifty states should enact laws that make it possible," Joan says.

She believes that coordinated databases will not only help to find offenders who have committed terrible crimes such as murder, but also help to find and save children at risk of becoming murder victims.

"The more we know about criminals the easier it becomes to prevent crimes. It is not only about solving," Joan notes. She also states that she would especially like to see Tennessee learn from other states. As an example she mentions that in Virginia offenders must serve at least 85 percent of their sentence, while in Tennessee they are eligible for parole after serving only 33 percent. As the mother of a murder victim Joan feels that the offenders should complete their entire sentence, as she believes that hard sentences will make people think before they commit crimes. As such, she is also in favour of capital punishment and will continue to fight for whatever she believes need changing.

"People say he got life, but they do not realise that the offender might be out on parole a few years later. And when we let murderers out on parole we put others' [lives] in jeopardy. We risk that they will commit murder again; it is all a matter of money. When murderers are let out it is simply because it is expensive keeping them in prison," Joan says.

As an activist Joan has also tried to influence how offenders are presented in court.

In 2015 Governor Bill Haslam of Tennessee signed the Victim Life Photo Bill into law, allowing murder victims to have an appropriate presence during trials. As president of the victim's rights group Hope for Victims, Joan coordinated support for the bill.

"It seems like criminals have more rights than the victims," Joan says. "They walk in to court dressed in beautiful clothes they probably don't even own. Meanwhile, we only see pictures of the victims from the crime scene or the autopsy. Victims have the right to have their face shown as we remember them before the crimes, because the jury needs to see the person they were before becoming [a] victim[.] The jury needs to see the happy and good person that was murdered, and this is what the offender should be convicted for. At the same time the offender should appear as they are and not be portrayed as better people in nice suits."

Joan feels there are too many cases where the public forgets who the real victims are— especially in death penalty cases. Not long ago, Joan was following the case of a man who was put on death row after he was convicted of raping and killing a seven-year-old girl. The media coverage upset Joan.

"When they finally put him to death it was all about him. Not the way he raped and killed the little girl and how her family will suffer forever. We have a tendency to focus on the perpetrator and not the victim. Therefore, I would never go to a [meeting] where the victim met the criminal. It would make me feel miserable, giving the criminal a chance of excusing himself and asking for forgiveness. When you commit a heinous crime you do not deserve that opportunity," Joan states candidly.

Over the years Joan has met a lot of politicians during the course of her lobbying. But she says laws are not about politics.

"It is about doing the right thing for the people who elected and trusted you. At times I feel I am fighting a losing battle. I have a grandchild that keeps me going. I want them to feel safe, and therefore it is worth the fight," Joan says.

She thinks that victims have more power than the general public to influence politicians because they have been impacted and affected by the crimes and therefore can share the consequences of criminal acts with them.

"People don't realise how the system works unless the crime happens to them. And the realisation is often disappointing," Joan says.

When asked if she would not have a more peaceful life if she left the lawmaking to others, Joan quickly replies that she cannot abandon her lobbying efforts, because someone needs to tell legislators that the justice system does not work. According to Joan, law enforcement agencies need the right laws and the right tools to make society safer, but legislators aren't providing them with these tools.

"Johnia wanted to make a difference in this world, and therefore I try to keep her memory alive by influencing lawmakers. And this way I also keep myself busy. I miss Johnia so much that it is good having this to attend to instead of just sitting down giving up," Joan says.

Today, Joan cries just as much as she did fourteen years ago. People often tell her she needs to move on, but Joan says there is no closure when your child is murdered. You just close one chapter to open another, she says.

"First chapter was to find the guy who killed Johnia. Next chapter was dealing with the justice system. All the time, a new chapter opens. It is so painful, and I would not wish this on my worst enemy," Joan says.

Besides struggling day to day just to get through, Joan also feels she has to struggle with simply being considered a normal person by other people. Because people treat you differently, she says, when they do not know what to say or how to react.

"People [would] rather turn around and walk away when they see you. They do not know if they should mention Johnia or if they should only talk about her. So many just keep silent. But I love to talk about Johnia, as she will always live in my heart, and people should not worry about making me sad. I already am, and I will be sad to the day that I die, so please just speak up with what's on your mind," Joan says.

She says that seeing people just paying attention and listening to her story gives her strength to carry on. The worst one can do, she says, is to pretend the crime never happened, because it did, and denying Johnia's memory means it's not being honoured as it deserves. Therefore, Joan loves when people tell her that she is in their prayers.

"I think prayers change lives," Joan says.

She says that believing in God and being a spiritual person has helped her through the hardest times. Often, she feels Johnia is still with her. For example, when she is driving she gets the feeling Johnia is sitting next to her. Somehow the air in the car just feels warmer. The same thing happens when Joan is alone in a room at night.

"I can feel her presence when she comes to visit. It is like she is always near. I talk a lot to her, and I often ask what she thinks about certain things. It helps, talking to her, and I thank God that I had her for more than twenty years," Joan says.

Besides affecting Joan's spiritual life her daughter's death has also influenced and encouraged her in every day life. For example, until recently she was unable to attend weddings.

"I could not [go] because it would remind me that I would never see Johnia get married. I also get really mad when I think about the fact that her killer's parents have a grandchild. I will never have Johnia's children in my life. I think it is unfair," Joan says, referring to the fact that Taylor Olson was a father when he committed suicide.

Joan is not angry at Taylor Olson's family. But she is still hurt by some of their actions. When Taylor Olson committed suicide his mother gave Joan her number and invited her to call and ask any questions she had regarding her son. Joan took up the offer and tried conversing with her, but the conversation ended quickly because Taylor Olson's mother defended her son, which caused Joan to become frustrated. She therefore hung up immediately. Because the call was not very long, Joan did not get the answers to her questions.

"I was also surprised and upset when I found out they had a remembrance page for him on Facebook," Joan says. "I looked at it and did not feel he deserved to be remembered."

Instead, she decided to turn the tables by honouring the victim's memory. When police had searched Johnia's apartment they found all the toys she had wrapped for the children. This inspired Joan and her husband, Michael, to lead an annual toy drive in their daughter's name. For thirteen years Joan has organised the Johnia Berry Memorial Toy Drive. Every year the foundation collects and distributes thousands of toys to needy children through schools and organisations in East Tennessee and Southwest Virginia. Joan describes the charity as "a heartwarming experience" and one that she does "in honour of Johnia and her love of children." Volunteers and sponsors at the local television station, WJHL, also dedicate their time to the cause. Every year for more than a month people and companies can drop off new, unwrapped toys for infants and children up to the age of fourteen years at Food City stores. The collection of toys always ends on the day of Johnia's murder, the sixth of December. Afterwards Joan and volunteers deliver the toys to children in need, so they get the help, and they experience the joy, Johnia tried to provide for children during the holiday season.

"It is a beautiful way of honouring Johnia's memory. She loved children and would be proud to see how we help them through the toy drive," Joan says.

She also believes that her daughter's death has brought her own family closer together. Every day she cherishes her husband, sons, and grandchildren. Joan knows how important it is to help others get through stressful situations and adapt to a new life. Three years ago Joan helped her sister when injustice struck her.

"Her son died a terrible death in a terrible accident. After losing Johnia I understood the pain she was going through. To me the most important thing is talking about the pain you feel. And even though your children pass away they are still alive in your heart, and what better way [to keep] them alive than talking about them," Joan says.

12

A VICTIM'S STATEMENT

All states allow victim impact statements—a chance for victims to describe how a crime has affected their lives. The statements are normally included in the presentencing report that the trial judge receives.

According to the National Center for Victims of Crime, the purpose of victim impact statements is:

> ...to allow crime victims, during the decision-making process on sentencing or parole, to describe to the court or parole board the impact of the crime. A judge may use information from these statements to help determine an offender's sentence; a parole board may use such information to help decide whether to grant a parole and what conditions to impose in releasing an offender. A few states allow victim impact information to be introduced at bail, pretrial release, or plea bargain hearings.

A victim impact statement may provide information about damage to victims that would otherwise have been unavailable to courts or parole boards. Victims are often not called to testify in court, and if they testify, they must respond to narrow, specific questions. Victim impact statements are often the victims' only opportunity to participate in the criminal justice process or to confront the offenders who have harmed them. Many victims report that making such statements improves their satisfaction with the criminal justice process and helps them recover from the crime.

(Source: *www.victimsofcrime.org*)

Although all states allow victim impact statements, too many victims never make such a statement, and too many perpetrators never go to court, **Rhonda Stapley** says. In 1974 she was abducted by one of the worst serial killers America has ever witnessed: Ted Bundy.

Rhonda miraculously escaped from the notorious killer, but afterwards she was too ashamed to come forward. Today, she feels guilty about the deaths of some of the girls Ted Bundy killed after he assaulted her. Her mission is to make victims speak up.

A VICTIM KEPT QUIET

Victim: Rhonda Stapley
Date of Birth: 08/19/1953
Missing From: Salt Lake City, Utah
Abducted: 11/10/1974 (21 years old)
Classification: Endangered Missing

Rhonda was watching the television show *M*A*S*H* when a news flash interrupted the sitcom. The anchor happily announced that law enforcement officers had finally got the man everyone had been talking about—and fearing. When the television station broadcast footage of the alleged abductor being brought in to the police station for questioning, Rhonda's roommate asked: "Which of them is the bad guy?"

The footage showed three men, all of whom looked the same in their street clothes. But Rhonda knew right away who the offender was. She had looked into his eyes one year earlier, on a beautiful autumn afternoon in Salt Lake City.

The sun had been shining and the weather was warmer than normal for that time of year. Rhonda hadn't enjoyed much of the day though. Earlier that Friday she'd had dental surgery, and her mouth had started to feel sore. The fourth-year pharmaceutical student knew she had to get back to campus quickly so she could take some aspirin, but the bus was more than half an hour late. So Rhonda decided to walk back to campus, cursing herself for putting on a new pair of hiking boots that were not yet broken in. The walk was going to be long and painful.

Just as she was about to leave the bus stop at Liberty Park, a car passed by slowly. After the car passed Rhonda, the driver stopped. He put the Volkswagen Beetle in reverse, and then he began to back up. A really good-looking guy rolled down the car window. In a calm, welcoming voice, he asked Rhonda where she was going. It turned out they were both heading to the University of Utah. The man gladly offered Rhonda a ride.

"It was a different time in the 1970s," Rhonda notes. "Crimes were committed, but in general people felt safe, and everyone helped each other. So getting into that car didn't seem a big risk, as it would today. It was just a friendly person offering a lift, like many friendly people did back then," Rhonda says.

Once she had climbed into the car she reached for the handle to close the door, but to her surprise it had been removed. However, she wasn't concerned. Instead, she focused on the driver.

The young and handsome man had curly dark hair and a friendly smile. Politely, he said he was a law student at the university…and as he shook Rhonda's hand he introduced himself as Ted.

Rhonda immediately found the articulate man interesting, but with her strict Mormon upbringing she felt no more than that. At the age of twenty-one years, she had never set foot in a bar. She was not dating, and her worst habit was consuming Pepsi-Cola.

"His eyes were bright," Rhonda remembers, "and I thought he was just a good-looking, kind student. We had a friendly and funny conversation, like students would have. We mainly spoke about college, and I felt comfortable. I thought he could be my next best friend."

For a while they drove towards the university; then Ted suddenly made a turn. When Rhonda noticed they were not taking the normal route to their destination, Ted asked whether it would be okay if he just ran a quick errand up by the zoo. Rhonda didn't mind, she was just happy that she had finally gotten a ride back home. But when they got to the zoo, Ted didn't stop. He continued towards Big Cottonwood Canyon, and when Rhonda asked why, Ted just replied the errand wasn't at the zoo, but near the zoo.

"Then suddenly he pulled over," Rhonda recalls. "It seemed like he was looking for a place to park. At this point I did not expect a murder attempt, I was more anticipating an attempt at a romantic parking episode, and I wasn't afraid of that either, just not interested, and wanting to get out of that potential situation without embarrassing either of us. I still thought he was a nice and somewhat charming guy right up to the moment," Rhonda says.

When Ted finally found a secluded parking spot between some trees, he turned around in the driver's seat and faced Rhonda directly. The shy girl was sure he was now going to try to kiss her, but when she looked into his eyes, she was in for a shock. The beautiful blue eyes had turned black and empty. And when Ted finally spoke again it was without affection.

"I am going to kill you," he said.

At first Rhonda thought it was a sick kind of humour, but when he grabbed her by the throat, she started to panic. Desperately she fought for her life, but she quickly lost her breath; shortly afterwards, she lost consciousness.

When she woke up again, Ted had put her on top of a picnic table and pulled her pants down in order to rape her.

"I was just begging for my life while he was beating me badly. He was shaking and slapping my head so wildly that the stitches from my dental surgery [were] ripped open. I had blood [over] my entire face and he started slugging me in the stomach. Then he choked me again till I lost consciousness, but he kept waking me up like he was playing a game. The last time he woke me up, he said '*Good girl! Don't die yet!*' and then he asked how I would actually like to die?" Rhonda recounts.

First, Ted imitated how he could cut off her air supply by putting his hand over her nose and mouth. Then, he visualised how he also could strangle her. Finally, he indicated, she had a third option: She could die by him sitting so hard on her body that she would no longer be able to breathe.

"He enjoyed torturing me, and then he choked me again—I think, this time with the intention of killing me," Rhonda recalls. "But I woke up, and I was now lying on the grass without him there. I could see he was standing by the car, moving some things in the back of it. It seemed he was removing the passenger seat so he could more easily move my corpse to a safer dumping ground. With him gone, I just got up and ran in the opposite direction, into the darkness."

However, she did not get far. Her trousers had been pulled down and were wrapped around her ankles. After a few steps she stumbled and fell into a fast-moving mountain stream.

"The river swept me away, and I think this saved my life. It was like a divine intervention, but then I felt the power of the river," Rhonda says.

For the next several minutes she was thrown about in the raging water. Again and again she was smashed into rocks. She started to panic.

"I thought that if he did not succeed [in] killing me, I was going to die by drowning," she recalls.

But once again Rhonda felt an intervention. She slammed into a pile of debris, causing her to stop. And although she was dazed, she fought her way back onto shore.

NOT THAT GIRL

For almost three hours Rhonda had been drifting in and out of consciousness, and she could not believe that her peaceful, religious life had turned into an inferno only a short while ago—a living Hell where she was being tortured by a human devil without any wrongdoing on her part. But as Rhonda pulled up her pants and started walking back towards Salt Lake City she could not help feeling ashamed.

"I didn't want to be the rape victim everyone talked about. I was afraid people would see me differently and treat me differently if they knew, and I felt embarrassed for having put myself in that situation. So I decided no one could know about what had happened," Rhonda explains.

She says that most people are taught never to go off with a stranger, that if you decide to do so in spite of the warnings, you often are automatically blamed for the offender's ensuing assault.

"The girl that is raped is often seen as the stupid girl that didn't listen. I didn't want to be that girl," Rhonda reiterates.

Being the victim of a sexual assault also collided with the tenets of Rhonda's strict Mormon upbringing. If people in her church community knew what had happened she would no longer be seen as 'pure'.

"And I was afraid my mother would force me to leave school and make me stay at home to protect me, but also because she would feel ashamed," Rhonda says.

The days following the attack were difficult to get through for Rhonda. She had a lot of bruises on her face; but instead of telling her friends the bruises were caused by her perpetrator, she lied and said they were the result of dental surgery. Somehow her friends believed her. The most difficult part, though, was coming to terms with her fear.

"He still had my backpack with my ID, so he knew who I was and where I lived. I was so scared he would come back for me, and that it would make him even angrier if I went to the police. So I kept quiet, like more than eighty percent of all rape victims do," Rhonda says.

Her silence meant she had to find ways of dealing with the effects of the trauma on her own. As is the case for many other victims, she found comfort through substance abuse. Soon the Mormon was addicted to prescription pills, and she became self-destructive. She felt her life no longer mattered.

"With my strict Puritan upbringing I was told the most important thing a young woman could have was her virtue. If she lost her virtue she might as well lose her life. I had now lost my virtue and, I felt, I no longer had value as a human being," Rhonda confides.

Shortly after the assault Rhonda dropped out of her church activities and began avoiding her family and friends. Instead, she self-medicated to numb the pain in her mind so she didn't have to think about what had happened every moment. Slowly, she also began to act reckless.

"I've never been an athletic runner, but after the assault I had so much nervous energy that I needed to run it off. At the same time other women went missing, so my roommates didn't think it was safe [being] out alone late at night, but I was not afraid of him getting me in the night. If he did, I was ready with my rat-tail comb and would not have hesitated the least in stabbing him. I would have killed him for what he had done to me," Rhonda says.

During the autumn of 1974, the media in Utah and the surrounding states continually reported on women who had vanished or who had been victims of an attempted abduction by a mysterious man driving a Volkswagen Beetle.

"In the beginning I truly thought the attack on me was an isolated incident. Today, I know it was not," Rhonda says.

Following the news reports, Rhonda learned that a week before "Ted" abducted her he was suspected of also having kidnapped and killed Nancy Wilcox, a sixteen-year-old student at Olympus High School. Just like Rhonda, Nancy Wilcox was active in the local Mormon

Church. The teenager disappeared when she went to buy a pack of gum. She was last seen riding in a Volkswagen Beetle, and even though police launched a massive search for Nancy Wilcox, they never found her.

"I could not have helped prevent a crime that took place before the one committed against me, but perhaps I could have saved Debra Kent," Rhonda reflects today.

A month after Rhonda was attacked, her predator abducted seventeen-year-old Debra Kent from the parking lot of Viewmont High School in Bountiful, Utah. Debra Kent was attending a play at the school and had left during intermission to pick up her brother, but she never returned.

"And I also feel guilty for what happened to Carol DaRonch," Rhonda says.

A few hours before Ted Bundy abducted Debra Kent, he attempted to abduct Carol DaRonch from the parking lot at a mall. Ted Bundy pretended to be a policeman, calling himself Officer Roseland. The false police officer explained that he had just apprehended a person who had tried to break in to Carol DaRonch's car. She agreed to come down to the station to close the case; but once she and "Officer Roseland" were underway in the Volkswagen Beetle, the driver tried to handcuff her. Carol DaRonch fought for her life. She finally managed to get out of the car and seek help from others.

Rhonda feels she perhaps could have saved Debra Kent's life and prevented the abduction of Carol DaRonch.

"When two girls where abducted on the same day, it made news all over Utah, and I followed the broadcasting closely, because I knew right away that my bad guy was their bad guy as well. I had hoped I was the only victim. Now, I knew, I was not. I felt it was my fault others had probably been killed, because I did not warn [anyone] about him. The feeling of guilt destroyed me," Rhonda says.

While she tried to accept that she could not undo her silence, law enforcement desperately tried to catch a killer on the loose.

THE OFFENDER ESCAPED

In the predawn hours of August 16, 1975, Utah Highway Patrol Officer Bob Hayward observed Rhonda Stapley's "Ted" cruising a residential area in a suburb of Salt Lake City. When the officer searched Ted's car he found a ski mask, a crowbar, handcuffs, an ice pick, a coil of rope, and other items typically used to commit burglaries. Ted was arrested. And when media outlets reported the apprehension, Rhonda learned the full name of her abductor, Ted Bundy.

At the police station, Ted Bundy explained that he had found the handcuffs in a Dumpster, and that he used the ski mask for skiing; but going through his explanation, Detective Jerry Thompson realised that the detainee fit the description of the suspect of Carol DaRonch's kidnapping. And so did Ted Bundy's car. Officers obtained a warrant to search his apartment, where they found an advertisement for the Viewmont High School play where Debra Kent had disappeared, and they found a guide to ski resorts in Colorado. In the guide there was a checkmark singling out the Wildwood Inn, a hotel four hundred miles south of Salt Lake City, where Caryn Campbell, a twenty-three-year-old nurse, had gone missing half a year earlier. Later, when her body was found, investigators determined Caryn had been killed by blows to her head from a blunt instrument. Collectively, however, the findings did not provide sufficient evidence to detain Ted Bundy. He was released.

Shortly afterwards, Ted Bundy sold his Volkswagen Beetle to a teenager. Law enforcement officers immediately impounded the car, and when technicians dismantled it they found hair matching samples from Caryn Campbell's body. The FBI also found strands of hair from other women—among them, Carol DaRonch.

On October 2, 1975, a year after the abduction of Rhonda Stapley, the FBI arranged a lineup to see whether a witness might corroborate their suspicions. Carol DaRonch immediately identified Ted Bundy as the man who had abducted her. The suspect was charged with aggravated kidnapping and attempted criminal assault. Ted Bundy's parents, however, quickly paid the $15,000 bail.

While awaiting trial, detectives from Utah and Colorado met to discuss the case. They quickly agreed that they needed more evidence before they also charged Ted Bundy with the murder of Caryn Campbell. So when the trial started in February 1976, Ted Bundy was charged with only the kidnapping of Carol DaRonch, as law enforcement could not confidently link him to either Caryn Campbell's murder or the murder of Debra Kent.

Ted Bundy was sentenced to fifteen years in prison in Utah, but shortly after the conviction, law enforcement officers in Colorado became convinced they had enough evidence to convict Ted Bundy of the murder of Caryn Campbell. Ted Bundy was extradited to the city of Aspen.

When the preliminary hearing began in June 1977, Ted Bundy decided to serve as his own attorney, which made it possible for him to appear in court in a suit, instead of wearing a prison uniform and shackles. During a recess he asked to use the courthouse's law library to research his case. But instead of conducting research, he opened the window and jumped from the second story. Shortly afterwards, his escape was public knowledge.

"It sent me right back to when I was assaulted," Rhonda recalls. "I thought that if he was smart enough to get out of prison, he was also smart enough to find me, and I developed an even greater abuse of sleeping pills," she says.

Ted Bundy was on the run for six days before he was finally arrested again when two police officers noticed a car weaving in and out of its lane before suddenly making a U-turn. When the officers pulled the driver over, they found Ted Bundy driving a stolen car.

Following his escape from the courthouse library, authorities decided to move the trial to Colorado Springs. But once again Ted Bundy outsmarted law enforcement. Most of the jail staff was on Christmas break when Ted Bundy piled books in his bed, covering them with a blanket so guards would think he was sleeping. Instead, he climbed into the crawl space; later, he broke through the ceiling to the apartment of the chief jailer, who was out having dinner with his wife. In the apartment, Ted Bundy stole civilian clothing. Afterwards, he got on a bus to Denver, where he bought an airplane ticket to Chicago.

Seventeen hours after his escape, when the jail staff discovered that Ted Bundy was gone, the suspect was already in the Windy City.

"I worked at a pharmacy at the corner of a cafe," Rhonda says, recounting her personal experience of the events that day. "They had the TV on, and suddenly someone came running, saying that Ted Bundy had escaped again. That was when I thought he was now gonna come after me to finish what he started. It was like a never-ending nightmare."

But Ted Bundy didn't come back to Utah. Instead, he travelled to Florida, where he resumed his attacks. This time the killing spree lasted two months before the wanted man was apprehended in Pensacola.

When Ted Bundy was tried for his crimes in Florida, he was convicted of one kidnapping and three murders before being sentenced to death. But it wasn't until ten years later, a few days before his execution in 1989, that he confessed to the murders of thirty women in six different states across America. However, the actual number of murders committed by Ted Bundy is unknown. It is suspected to be much higher than thirty.

Among the women Ted Bundy admitted to having killed was Nancy Wilcox. The serial killer confessed to having abducted her at knifepoint in Salt Lake City, when she went to buy gum. Afterwards, he sexually assaulted the teenager in a nearby orchard. Then he strangled her and buried her body near Capitol Reef National Park, almost two hundred miles from where she went missing in Utah. Despite his confession, law enforcement has never been able to locate Nancy Wilcox's remains.

FEELING GUILTY

However, in 2015 law enforcement officers found another person's remains, prompting police to look through their missing persons files. By using DNA testing, law enforcement identified the remains as those of Debra Kent, whom Ted Bundy had confessed to having abducted and murdered before his execution. The serial killer had also confessed to killing several other women who had died in or around Salt Lake City during the months when Rhonda had been abducted. All of them, including Rhonda, had one thing in common: They were petite and had long brown hair, which they wore parted down the middle.

Today, Rhonda no longer hides the fact that she feels guilty about what happened to some of the victims.

"In the beginning I felt I had no more to add to the investigation, and I excused myself for not having come forward. But when I learned who he was and that others had become victims after me, I felt guilty. This guilt has reappeared several times. When he escaped, I also felt guilty, because he was gonna murder again. Today, I wish I had reported him, and perhaps I would have been able to save some of the victims," Rhonda acknowledges.

No matter how hard she tries, Rhonda is never able to erase Ted Bundy from her memories. She is constantly reminded of the pain he inflicted on her. Both mentally and physically. Rhonda suffers from post-traumatic stress disorder (PTSD). She has received treatment for the condition for years.

"I have a numbness in my thighs. Especially when I get nervous, they go numb. I think it comes from when he sat on my legs to cover my nose and mouth. I also suffer from constant noise in my ears, and when the rain runs down the gutters it triggers it for me. It reminds me of the raging river next to the site where he abused me," Rhonda says.

However, the traumatic effects of the assault are not only physical. Since Rhonda was abducted she has also felt an anger she cannot explain the origins of. And although she accepts that most people are good, she still suspects that everyone is capable of becoming evil. And the PTSD also affects how she acts during everyday situations.

"I prefer going to my car when there is no one around. If I see people in the parking lot at the mall, I always go back into the shops till I can see the lot is empty again," Rhonda confides.

Getting treatment has helped in certain situations. Rhonda is no longer bothered by heavy rains to the same degree she used to be. The change came after she went back to the crime scene accompanied by her therapist.

"When we got there I right away recognised the sound of the river. Being there, and now knowing why I have always been disturbed by rain, was a big step forward. It made me think about that it is not the river, the canyons, or the site of the attack that represented a danger. It was the monster—and he is gone forever," Rhonda says.

The assault has also affected how Rhonda associates with other people. One of the reasons she was waiting for the bus on the day she was taken was because she did not like driving her own car; therefore she left it on campus when she went to the dentist. Today, however, she is fanatic in terms of having to drive the car.

"I have become a control freak, and I don't trust others with driving. I also want to be the one who pays the bills at home, the one who delegates the assignments at work—and everything has to go through me. When I am in control, I feel more protected, and I just have an issue with not trusting others," Rhonda admits.

However, a situation in which she was not in control finally convinced Rhonda to come forward and tell someone about the afternoon Ted Bundy tried to kill her.

In 2012, the pharmacy where Rhonda worked had to let people go. As a result, Rhonda had a clash with her boss. Rhonda says her supervisor wanted to replace highly paid, long-standing pharmacists with fresh-out-of-college graduates, so the pharmacy could pay them less. And Rhonda was not afraid to tell her boss that no one deserved to be fired.

"He yelled at me and used the same intonation and viciousness as Ted Bundy had when he attacked me. The verbal abuse brought back all the bad memories—and, not least, the PTSD. After the clash, I started having panic attacks, and I suffered from insomnia. I had this feeling I was going crazy," Rhonda explains.

Without her family's knowledge, Rhonda attended counseling sessions, trying to control both her fear and inner anger. It was not until one of her two daughters made a joke that Rhonda finally revealed to her family what had happened forty years earlier.

Together with her daughters, who wishes to remain anonymous, Rhonda had gone to get some fast food. Annoyed with waiting for the food, Rhonda made one of her frequent, angry outbursts, leading to her daughter joking that she should see a therapist. Immediately, Rhonda told the daughters that she already was. The news came much to the daughters' surprise.

"My daughters reacted with disbelief when I finally told [them] what had happened. They were in shock, but they were also proud that I finally dared to share my story with others. I think they were relieved to know, because they had firsthand experienced how my PTSD had affected me and the family over the years. Now they had an explanation," Rhonda says.

A SECRET PAIN

Three years after Ted Bundy's attack on her, Rhonda met her husband, Barry. Rhonda immediately told him that she had previously been raped, but she never went into details about the assault, and her husband never asked.

"He accepted who I was, and he said that it did not matter to him what had happened. He was just interested in supporting me and starting a new life together," Rhonda explains.

Now Barry and the daughters had a full explanation of Rhonda's past, and how it affected her present. She then decided to write a book, titled *I Survived Ted Bundy: The Attack, Escape & PTSD that Changed My Life*. Rhonda says that writing the book is the best decision she ever made, because it worked as therapy, forcing herself to go through the assault all over and driving her to structure her thoughts.

"I have freed myself by writing that book. As a victim you think you are the only person who [has] suffered this. It was your experience, and you feel alone with it; but when you open up you find out there are others who have suffered the same. You almost find some kind of camaraderie with other victims that will make you move forward from being a victim to a survivor. I found that camaraderie when publishing the book," Rhonda says.

However, getting the book published was not easy, because many publication houses were afraid people would accuse them—and Rhonda—of telling a lie.

"Some doubted my trustworthiness, because I had kept silent for so many years, and there was no police report to confirm my story. But most victims of rape and abuse keep silent. They do not go to the police, and my intention [in] writing the book has also been to hopefully help victims have the courage to share their stories and begin their healing journey as it is difficult to heal if you just hold all the pain inside secretly," Rhonda says.

She hopes that sharing stories of abuse will in some cases also help prevent others from becoming victims. And, not least in her mind, she hopes it will shed light on how many victims there are.

"The feeling of loneliness is a deep, horrible state of mind, and it is important, sharing your story, and reaching out to others. Knowing you are not alone gives comfort, and it is easier to regain trust in others if you have the help of others," Rhonda notes.

She also believes that the more stories that are shared the greater an understanding people will obtain of what being a victim is like. Rhonda says that today people often wrongfully accuse victims of having self-inflicted their abuse.

"[I]t does not matter if the victim has been drinking, if the victim has been walking alone, or what the victim has been wearing. It is never the victim's fault," Rhonda says.

To avoid self-guilt—and to create a beautiful life even after becoming the victim of a predator—Rhonda suggests victims always seek professional help immediately after the assault. After having suffered from her trauma for forty-five years, Rhonda says she believes that the effects due to PTSD, in some cases, can feel worse than the actual assault.

"I would suggest that you as a victim contact a psychologist right away. A psychologist can even help you [go] to the police. But never conceal what happened to you. If you open up, you'll often have the entire support of your community. If you keep it to yourself, you won't have any help at all, and your offender will keep creating victims, just like my offender did," Rhonda says.

EPILOGUE
A LETTER OF HOPE

by Mary Kozakiewicz

Dear Reader,

This may have been a difficult book for you to read, due to the heavy—and often heartbreaking—content. Your child may have gone missing, or may have been recovered. You may be a survivor. You may have picked up this book to discover tips regarding how to keep your own family safe. Or perhaps you were merely curious about what it is like to live through every parent's worst nightmare.

Our children are precious, irreplaceable, and the centre of our universe. Children give us purpose and reason. To lose them, in any manner, is unthinkable.

I know this all too well, because the little girl, Alicia, who is featured in the first chapter, is my child. Or at least she was.

That little girl is now an adult, and she is *so* strong. She fills my heart with pride and is my hero. Actually, *hero* is the perfect word to describe her. She works to prevent crimes against children and seeks to provide aid in their rescue and healing. This is her passion and her life's mission. It has been her focus for sixteen years. She is an advocate, motivational speaker, and survivor. Recently, her impact reached to new heights: She joined the International Centre for Missing and Exploited Children (ICMEC) as the Director of Outreach and Global Impact. Alicia, and the entire ICMEC team, are dedicated to crafting miracles for children around the world.

These miracles do happen, but heartbreakingly, only for some. Families do move forward, with varying success, but it's not all luck. It's fate—yes, fate—and, barring that, it's hard work, determination, and tears.

So many tears.

When your child is recovered safely, it may be the happiest day of your life. It also may be the most harrowing. Initially, there is an intense joy. The nightmare has ended, and your miracle actually happened! All of the prayers, posters, phone calls, hard work, and, most importantly, tireless and boundless hope, helped to bring your child home. In my family's case, before Alicia was returned to us law enforcement shared that the chance of Alicia being recovered alive was a million to one.

Think about that, a million to one.

We won the lottery.

This lottery, though won, was not the one we played. The child who returned, our princess, was not quite the child she had been. However, neither were we, her family.

Trauma changes us. It shakes our core. Not only in major, earth-shattering ways, but also in the tiny day-to-day moments that make up our lives. Predators sometimes do not only physically steal our children. In our case, the predator stole, through nearly a year of grooming, her heart and soul, her ability to reason, and even her childhood memories—her past. This also took our future; at least, the future we believed we would have. I still grieve for my child and the life that I lost.

Today, though, I rejoice in the future we have built in spite of the struggles. We, through hard work, love, and the will to continue, made it. However, it was not easy. It's amazing how quickly everything can change.

In a millisecond, the blink of an eye, a family can be destroyed. Whatever the circumstances of your child's disappearance, it is true that nothing will ever be quite the same. Once you've survived the devastation of your own Ground Zero, that ground never again will promise the stability you had previously counted on. For the families who have experienced this trauma, the next quake—and the subsequent, oncoming explosions—are forever imminent. Parents who have lost their children, no matter the duration or outcome, are no longer unaware of the existence of pure evil.

You may feel hopeless…lost in the storm with no direction or path to follow. So, what can we do to find our way?

The expectation cannot, and should not, be to immediately "bounce back". It does not seem possible to survive such an event and simply move forward. We do just that—we move forward—sometimes slowed to a crawl—each at our own pace. But, we move…and we keep on moving. It's okay if it's 100 steps forward and 99 steps back. The pitfalls may be many, as that landscape of our existence has forever been altered. I have certainly fallen into my share of emotionally and physically exhausting pits, and I have helped to pull my daughter from hers as well. We do this by being supportive, and by standing together. Love, and the hope for a better tomorrow, must be constant. It all starts with that first step in the right direction.

What are the first, and most crucial steps, we can take when we first discover our child is missing? We do the impossible—and we can—because nothing is impossible when it comes to the safety of our children. We strive to keep it together, knowing that we are our child's best advocate. We have to try to take deep breaths and stay focused, because time is of the essence. Our children might be moving away from us at the rate of 60 MPH. The rate our children are separated from us will be even faster if the child is moved from a car to an airplane.

When your child is missing, you need to call emergency services and law enforcement immediately. Do not hesitate, and do not wait twenty-four hours. There is no easy way to say this next sentence. Statistically, here in the United States, in the case of an abductor with homicidal inclinations, children are typically murdered within three hours of their abduction.

You need to locate your child's most recent photograph. Perhaps it is a school photo. Please, just be certain that it is not highly edited or filtered. Compile a list of friends, family, neighbours, schools, and anywhere your child spends their time. It is also important to consider all relationships. Are you separated or divorced from your child's other parent? Call them. Now.

After you establish that your child is indeed missing, contact the 24/7 call centre at the National Center for Missing and Exploited Children (NCMEC). The number is 1-800-THE-LOST (1-800-843-5678). The centre has translators and people waiting on the line to assist you. Supply the centre with the picture of your child and all relevant information, so that they can coordinate with any authorities and create a "Missing Child" poster to be shared throughout the community, and the world. These posters *do* bring our children home. An NCMEC poster helped to bring Alicia home, and the posters have helped in the recovery of so many other children as well.

It is also essential to cooperate with law enforcement, be it local police or federal authorities. Media is an effective tool, but can become overwhelming. Use it, but be cautious, sharing only relevant information. Often, it is best to appoint one trusted family member to speak on your behalf. Do not be afraid to ask for, and be willing to accept, help from family, friends, or whomever might be willing and able to assist you. Many people may want to help, but they may not feel comfortable reaching out and asking you. It will be so much harder to go through this alone.

After you have done all that you can…you wait. Time ceased to exist while Alicia was missing. The days rolled into nights and slipped slowly back into days. This passage of time barely registered. To me, it felt like one excruciatingly long day. During this period, I neither ate nor slept. How could I eat or sleep when my child was quite possibly in the hands of a monster? She could be cold, hungry, hurting, and terrified—or worse. The "worst" is what you struggle to contain below the surface of consciousness, never wanting to make that reality a possibility. I knew that once I allowed myself the freedom to consider the worst, I would cease to function.

Friends came to my house and offered whatever assistance they could. They attempted to engage me, and to ease my pain. They were angels of mercy when I could allow myself none. When Alicia was recovered, they offered support, while I was unraveling what had transpired. Alicia was one of the first children to be groomed and abducted by an internet predator. No one understood the grooming process, and ultimately, both my daughter and our family were blamed, rather than the predator.

How?

By convincing themselves that Alicia was a "bad child", and that my husband and I were "bad parents," a terrified public could excuse themselves from accepting responsibility for their own inadequacies on the subject. Due to the intense media coverage, we found ourselves unable to leave the house without a sometimes hostile public pointing their collective finger at us.

Alicia, already severely traumatised from the abduction, was now traumatised by the environment surrounding her. This environment was her home, her community—it should have been a safe and comforting place for her to return to. This created new complications in the healing process. Alicia would walk with her shoulders hunched, and her head down—the stature of a victim—when she was confronted by others. She experienced what no victim ever should—shame for what had been done to her.

This was not at all acceptable, but it also was unavoidable. We had to learn to cope and determine appropriate responses. I shared with Alicia that the best revenge was to be happy. Alicia changed her stance—she stood straight and tall, with her shoulders back. She would look the detractors directly in their eyes and simply give them a wide smile. This helped her to gain her footing and grow her confidence. It was amazing how quickly the cowards would back down and then assume the same head-down posture themselves.

You may need to prepare yourselves, and your child, for this sort of public behaviour. Often, it may be those you would least expect who become the loudest detractors. Realise it's their fear, but realise that it can also be jealousy. No, seriously. There are those who live such narrow, small-minded little lives that, despite the agonies that your child and family have endured, they will begrudge you what attention you may have received through the media. You're now, in their misguided opinion, famous, and they are not. Alicia was confronted with this mindset by her peers. Unbelievable. There were times when Alicia would share her story, and although the children in the audience understood her pain, they felt it would be worth it to go through something similar, simply for the "fame".

It is also important to remember that although some may be cruel, there are people who would love to offer kind words and support. Do not misjudge the good, and good-natured, people, based on a few truly terrible people. It is often human nature to focus on the negative. Try not to let the terrible people continue to darken your days.

As Alicia and I moved forward, working tirelessly to educate the public, my peers would accuse me of living vicariously through my child. Ironically, *my* mission was *their* children's safety.

A piece of advice: Walk away from those who refuse to see beyond themselves and from those who do not have the courage to be there for you as you need them, and to love and support you despite public opinion. Stare them down, or simply try to ignore them. Your child, and your family, require positive support in order to heal.

Returning to school was yet another hurdle for Alicia. I had home-schooled her for the remainder of the year following her recovery, in order to allow her the time to heal, and also to protect her from the public. Learning is difficult when one is experiencing flashbacks, post-traumatic stress disorder, insomnia, and memory loss, yet we persevered. Alicia returned to public school for her freshman year. I encouraged her to join every activity that interested her, and to engage in public service. She created the Alicia Project, at fourteen years old, just about a year after her rescue, and began to give presentations, teaching her peers how to stay safe in the online world and off. She had given what happened to her a purpose, and that purpose is to save other children, and families, from experiencing a similar ordeal.

Despite a myriad of social, emotional, and educational issues, Alicia graduated from high school with honours. It was a huge accomplishment, but nobody saw the nights that I tutored her into the wee hours of the morning in order to relearn what she had lost due to amnesia. Nobody saw the tears forming at the cruel words of her peers. Yet again, we persevered, and held our heads high. I would remind her: You just have to study until you ace the test. Smile at your detractors until they back down. Ignore the ignorance because it is just that, and it is beneath you.

That's the secret. Support your child tirelessly and expect them to succeed, not just adequately, but superlatively. They have been traumatised, and it may be harder for them in some areas, but they are not destroyed. They've survived hell, and so have you. You are both stronger than you think. You can do this. With your unconditional love and support, your child can accomplish anything! As far as education, I am proud to share that Alicia went on to get her master's degree in forensic psychology.

The struggles of surviving trauma are not simple, and are not always expected. Over the years, Alicia and I have found ourselves in rooms filled with families who are still searching, or whose children have been recovered deceased. I remember the first conference where this occurred. Alicia and I were both overwhelmed by "survivor's guilt". This was an emotion for which we were not prepared. We did receive a miracle, and are grateful beyond words. But, why us? Why were we so lucky?

Every child, every family, deserves that same miracle. We are unable to change the past, but we have made it our life's mission to create a safer world tomorrow for all children.

We parents, the "moms of the missing", if you will, stand together, and pray when a child is missing, celebrate when a child is found safe, and mourn when a child is recovered deceased. We are part of a club that no one would choose to join, but we members are here for each other, for it is so much harder to go through it alone. Many of those featured in this book have been members, alongside myself, of various organisations dedicated to protecting children, and supporting the families of the missing and exploited. I have listened to their stories, celebrated their victories, and have shared their grief. NCMEC hosts an incredible group of these parents who volunteer themselves as support structures for other families, as shoulders to cry on, and as someone who truly understands the sheer terror others who are sharing our nightmare may be experiencing. I was one of those parents and received great comfort, support, and advice while Alicia was missing. I am proud to have been a member of this team for fifteen years. Together, we are Team HOPE—and offering hope, healing, and peace is what we do.

Alicia's story is a message of hope for the families who are still searching for their children. It is the hope that *every* child can be returned safely home.

Yours sincerely,
Mary Kozakiewicz

AUTHOR'S NOTE

As the author of *Moms of the Missing: Living the Nightmare* it is my hope that this book will help readers understand the extreme pain the victims suffer from these horrific crimes and, as importantly, raise awareness about how these abductions may occur. My deepest hope, however, is that by telling the stories of the victims we may help some of the missing persons return home. Someone knows something, and we hope they will come forward with information leading to the recovery of the missing person. By putting the focus on these types of crimes—which are committed against both children and adults—we can also hope to help prevent others from becoming victims. Here are some ways to keep your child and loved ones safe.

WAYS TO PREVENT ABDUCTIONS!

Online Safety

Many children are lured by online predators. Be aware of your child's activity in chat rooms (for example), and who they communicate with online. The predators often present themselves as being kids.

Furthermore, talk to your children about online safety, and tell them never to give out personal information. And remember yourself not to post photos of your children that can identify them and their whereabouts to strangers. Be aware that children often trust adults who know their names, so do not give that away.

Here are some guidelines developed by survivor Alicia Kozakiewicz.

- *Any child or teen can become the victim of an internet predator.*

- *Teach your child or teen to never share private or identifying information with a person online who is not known or trusted in real life.*

- *Strengthen the privacy settings on all social networking sites on every device in your household, and ensure that these settings remain unchanged after updates.*

- *Remind your child or teen to choose an online handle, username, or screen name carefully.*

- *Monitor your child's or teen's activity and know their passwords on your home computer and on all mobile devices.*

- *If you suspect your child or teen is being cyberbullied: Be supportive, get the facts, and, if necessary, contact your school or law enforcement. Conversely, teach your child or teen that there are negative consequences for those who cyberbully.*

- *Educate yourself on the mobile applications your child or teen is using. Ask for an explanation and a demonstration.*

- *Maintain loving, open, and respectful lines of communication with your child or teen while setting enforceable rules for online safety.*

- *If you feel that your child or teen is being groomed, harassed, threatened, or exploited online, you should immediately report this activity to your local law enforcement agency and the National Center for Missing and Exploited Children's CyberTipline.*

For further information visit: www.aliciakozak.com

Physical Protection

Talk to your child about how to behave and take care of themselves in public places such as malls, parks, public bathrooms, and similar areas. And make sure you have an agreement about which public places your children can go to.

Make sure you are also very careful when choosing babysitters, nannies, and childcare providers. Check their backgrounds and references.

Tell your children never to accept candy or gifts from strangers. And never to go with a stranger. Often, predators ask a child for help finding an animal.

Teach your child that he or she should scream and call for help if a stranger tries to grab them, follows them, or tries to force them into a car.

Tell your children that it is always okay for them to tell you if they have had bad experiences, even if another adult has told them not to.

Talk to your child about what to do if they get lost in a store or at the mall. Instruct them always to ask a cashier for help.

Show your children where friends live around the neighbourhood so they know where to go if they need help.

Make sure your children know what cars they can ride in. Teach them always to step away if a car and a driver they do not know pulls up to them.

Family Abductions

According to the National Center For Missing and Exploited Children, parents can take a number of preventative steps if they fear their child is in danger of being abducted by a family member. Among other steps, the centre recommends:

- *Obtaining a custody determination from the appropriate court that specifically outlines custody and visitation rights.*

- *Requesting that the judge include abduction-prevention measures in a description of the visitation rights; these measures include supervised visitation, posting a bond, entering a child's name in the Passport Issuance Alert Program, and surrendering a child's passport to the court.*

- *Advising the child's school or day care centre of custody orders. Flag passport applications for your child, and have children memorise essential information, such as home address and phone number, in case of emergencies.*

(Source: *www.missingkids.org*)

GET HELP!

It is easier to solve an abduction case when parents can provide law enforcement agencies with exact information about their children's height, weight, and eye colour, along with a recent photograph of the child.

Additionally, make sure that you as the parent of your children keep your children's medical and dental cards up to date. This can help solve the crime. Having your children fingerprinted can also be helpful. Many police departments sponsor fingerprinting. If your child is in danger of being abducted by a family member, it is a good idea to make sure custody documents are in order.

If your child is missing, the National Center for Missing and Exploited Children recommends you do the following:

Immediately call your local law enforcement agency.

After you have reported your child missing to law enforcement, call the National Center for Missing and Exploited Children at 1-800-THE-LOST (1-800-843-5678).

If your child is missing from home, search through:

- Closets.
- Piles of laundry.
- In and under beds.
- Inside large appliances.
- Vehicles—including trunks.
- Anywhere else that a child may crawl or hide.

If your child cannot be found in a store:

Notify the store manager or security office.

Then immediately call your local law enforcement agency. Many stores have a Code Adam plan of action in place.

When you call law enforcement:

- Provide law enforcement with your child's name, date of birth, height, weight, and descriptions of any other unique identifiers, such as eyeglasses and braces. Tell them when you noticed your child was missing and what clothing he or she was wearing.

- Request law enforcement authorities immediately enter your child's name and identifying information into the FBI's National Crime Information Center Missing Person File.

Help for Parents of Missing Children!

Team HOPE is a group of ordinary people who one day were forced to live every parent's nightmare; We have all experienced the trauma of having a missing or exploited child. We know the pain, fear, frustration, and loneliness that comes with having a missing or sexually exploited child. Armed with this knowledge and experience, we are dedicated to offering compassionate peer support, empathy, understanding, kindness, and friendship to families who are still searching, have recovered their children safely, have located their children deceased, and families with children who have been sexually exploited. We are here to provide hope and walk the journey with other families.

Do you have a missing or sexually exploited child? Unsure of what to do?

Call 866-305-HOPE (4673) to talk to a Team HOPE member.

(*Excerpted from: www.missingkids.org*)

Volunteers!

Team HOPE volunteers are the heart and soul of Team HOPE. They have demonstrated an incredible ability to turn personal tragedies into vital support for other families. We have volunteers in almost every state and from all walks of life. Volunteers are screened and attend in-depth trainings before they are matched with a family to support. All peer-support is telephone-based.

Team HOPE's trained volunteers:

- Help families in crisis with a missing, sexually exploited, or recovered child as they handle the day-to-day issues of coping and/or searching for their child.

- Help provide peer and emotional support, compassion, coping tools, and empowerment to families with missing, sexually exploited, and recovered children.

- Help instill courage, determination, and hope in parents and other family members.

- Help alleviate the feelings of isolation so often resulting from fear and frustration.

(Excerpted from: www.missingkids.org)

ACKNOWLEDGEMENTS

Special thanks to all the brave participants for telling your important stories. Hopefully, this will help prevent other abductions and, just as importantly, help your loved ones find their way home. Someone knows something…I admire your strength to keep fighting and your ability to maintain hope even though every parent's worst nightmare has become your reality. Also, thank you very much Claus Krogh, Lindsey Mesa, Gemma Taylor, Felix Mesa, and my family for your support and great advice while writing this book.

To Sophia and Benjamin.

SOURCES

This book is based on personal interviews with all participants.

I have gathered additional information and background knowledge from court records and other sources such as: The National Center for Missing and Exploited Children, the U.S. Department of Justice, the Federal Bureau of Investigation, The Surviving Parents Coalition, The Charley Project, the Polly Klass Foundation, the National Human Trafficking Hotline, the Polaris Project, the Global Slavery Index, ECPAT-USA, the Office of Juvenile Justice and Delinquency, the National Coalition Against Domestic Violence, The Doe Network, the United Nations, Child Find of America, the Child Rescue Network, the National Children's Alliance, RAINN, Childhelp, KidsHealth, the *Washington Post*, the *Los Angeles Times*, the *New York Post*, the *New York Times*, the *Boston Globe*, the *Chicago Tribune*, the *Miami Herald*, *Fulton Sun*, the *Knoxville News Sentinel*, *Huffington Post*, the *Orange County Register*, the *Atlanta Journal-Constitution*, the *Guardian*, BBC, CBS, NBC, Fox News, ABC, and CNN.

ABOUT THE AUTHOR

Steffen Hou (born 1975) is a Danish author and filmmaker. As a true crime author he has written about topics such as innocent Americans on death row, human trafficking, and the white supremacy movement. *Moms of the Missing: Living the Nightmare* is his third book.

Besides writing books and making documentary movies, Steffen also produces "The Deprived Podcast", which looks into various American crime stories, always with the intent of giving the victims a voice.

Read: www.steffenhou.com

Listen: www.deprivedpodcast.com